Love to
X

The FRIENDSHIP BOOK

of Francis Gay

D. C. THOMSON & CO., LTD.
London Glasgow Manchester Dundee

A Thought For Each Day In 1980

Sweet are the thoughts that savour of content;
The quiet mind is richer than a crowne.
Robert Greene (1558-92)

JANUARY

TUESDAY—JANUARY 1.

WHEN Ruth and Gerard told their respective families that they wanted to get married on New Year's Eve they met with a hostile reception. What a ridiculous time to choose for a wedding! Just after Christmas, with the likelihood of bitterly cold weather, and difficult travelling for the many guests coming from a distance.

But the wedding arrangements went ahead and, as it happened, the weather was mild and the day gilded by an hour or two of winter sunshine. They are a romantic couple, and they achieved their hearts' desire — to start the New Year together as man and wife. When you come to think of it the vows they made would make good New Year resolutions for any of us . . . to love, to honour, to be faithful . . . for better, for worse, for richer for poorer, in sickness and in health . . . A wonderful pledge with which to start 1980.

WEDNESDAY—JANUARY 2.

DR SAMUEL JOHNSON, the great 18th century wit and man of letters, was deeply religious and he compiled a number of prayers for his personal use. Here is the one he said at New Year:

" Almighty God, who hast safely brought me to the beginning of another year, and by prolonging my life dost invite me to repentance, forgive me that I have misspent the time past, enable me from this instant to amend my life . . . and grant me Thy Holy Spirit that I may so pass through things temporal as finally to gain things eternal, through Jesus Christ our Lord, Amen.

THE FRIENDSHIP BOOK

Thursday—January 3.

P. G. WODEHOUSE, whose light-hearted novels give pleasure to millions, used to tell how, when his mother's birthday was drawing near, she would drop hints of what she wanted, and his father, who loved her deeply, would act accordingly. The gift would be presented and would be accepted by his mother with as much delight as if it were something quite unexpected.

But one year she fancied a special pair of shoes, and for once his father was baffled. How could he possibly get the right size? So this was what they did. The mother went to the shop and bought the shoes, had them wrapped and took them home. She handed them to her husband, who put them in the usual place for "surprises" until the birthday arrived.

On that day husband presented wife with a beautifully-wrapped parcel. She opened it as if she had never seen it before, and, with many expressions of delight, tried on the shoes. More delight when she found they were a perfect fit. How clever her husband had been to know!

Does this strike you as rather silly? It didn't seem that way to the son, P. G. Wodehouse, who always remembered the simple delight the couple had in giving pleasure to each other.

And, after all, that, really, is what the giving of presents is all about, isn't it?

Friday—January 4.

THE philanthropist Samuel Warren once remarked, "There are two kinds of persons in the world—those who think first of difficulties, and those who think first of the importance of accomplishment *in spite of* difficulties."

THE FRIENDSHIP BOOK

Saturday—January 5.

SOUND advice about human relationships — and useful material for New Year resolutions — caught my eye in what at first might seem an unlikely source, the "600 Magazine," published for machine tool manufacturers and engineers.

The six most important words: "I admit I made a mistake."

The five most important words: "You did a good job."

The four most important words: "What is your opinion?"

The three most important words: "If you please."

The two most important words: "Thank you."

The least important word: "I."

Sunday—January 6.

THOU shalt love thy neighbour as thyself.

Monday—January 7.

THE death of Lady Churchill at the age of 92 signified in every way the passing of a great lady. When the long years of widowhood had taken their toll of her financial resources she quietly decided to sell some of her family treasures. When this became known it was suggested that, as a token of the nation's gratitude to Sir Winston's widow, she be given a special state pension. Lady Churchill, however, would not hear of this and continued with the sale.

At a time when many people are only too ready to grab all they can get, Lady Churchill retained her dignified independence to the end. Sir Winston would have been proud of her!

THE FRIENDSHIP BOOK

TUESDAY—JANUARY 8.

THE way to contentment is to learn how to accept what we can't alter. Let me tell you how this lesson was brought home to me, even if only in a small way.

The Lady of the House and I were staying with friends in the country. It had been snowing for two days and when it stopped I volunteered to take our friends' dog for a walk.

I was soon wishing I hadn't, for it started to rain and I was ankle-deep in slush. I was feeling very sorry for myself when, as I passed a gate, I saw a shepherd carrying two newly-born lambs and driving their mother to shelter.

" Terrible day!" I called to him.

" Terrible," he shouted back. " But it's an act of God. We can't do anything about it."

He was soaked to the skin and I was still dry, but he was so cheerful he made me feel ashamed.

I can't say the weather got any better after that, but, thinking about what he had said, I actually began to enjoy my walk!

WEDNESDAY—JANUARY 9.

JOSEPH TURNER was one of the world's great landscape painters. And I can tell you why. The clue is in a small footnote to his picture *Snow Storm* in the National Gallery in London. The inscription reads, " The artist was in this storm."

Turner said, " I wanted to show what such a scene was like. I got the sailors to lash me to the mast to observe it. I was lashed there for four hours, and I did not expect to escape."

With such dedication, no wonder his paintings are admired today, as much by experts as by ordinary people, just as they were in his lifetime.

QUIET HAVEN

I like to see within a harbour,
Little boats wait patiently,
As they did on ancient waters,
By the Sea of Galilee.

DAVID HOPE

THE FRIENDSHIP BOOK

Thursday—January 10.

SOME joy, some friends, some warmth of heart,
  A chance to lend a hand,
Some health, some strength to bear my part
  In the pattern God has planned.
These I would humbly ask, that I
  In my small corner here,
May light a candle, shed a glow
  Throughout the coming year.

Friday—January 11.

WE cannot all do great deeds, but we can all try to make the world a happier place. I'm thinking as I write of Johnnie Sutherland. After serving in the Middle East in the war, Johnnie returned to Thurso in the north of Scotland where he became a bus conductor. Not, you might think, a job that offers a man a path to any great renown. But it did to Johnnie. For he had perhaps the finest gift of all, a truly happy nature. If your face was gloomy when you came aboard, Johnnie had just the right word to cheer you up. If you'd a heavy message bag to cart from bus to cottage, Johnnie would notice, have a word with the driver, then carry it right to your door.

In off-duty hours he would drift down to the harbour, where he'd cheerfully charm, or buy some fish from the boats to drop in as an unexpected treat for a pensioner's tea.

Johnnie died after a short illness. One tribute— and he received many—would have pleased him particularly. I heard it from a man who travelled on Johnnie's bus for years. He was often surprised, he said, to find it raining when he stepped off the bus, it had seemed so sunny inside. A tribute, indeed.

THE FRIENDSHIP BOOK

Saturday—January 12.

I LIKE this story from a young mother who found her five-year-old son doing something he shouldn't have been.

"Goodness me," she said "What would Grannie think if I told her about you?"

"Oh," he replied, nothing daunted, "she can think what she likes. But she can't say anything to me. She's *your* mother, not mine!"

Sunday—January 13.

I AM the way, the truth, and the life.

Monday—January 14.

VIOLET HALL, of Calne, Wiltshire, sent me these lovely lines which she titles "The Homecoming."

The hour of day I like the best
Is when the sun sinks in the west;
For then my man comes home to me,
And I forget all else but he.

The irksome tasks, the things gone wrong,
Are whisked away on wings of song;
They vanish swiftly through the door,
As soon as my man's home once more.

The lamp aglow, the meal prepared,
Our troubles halve as soon as shared;
And Bill sits toasting slippered feet,
Then takes his old accustomed seat.

The dishes cleared, now time is ripe
For Bill to light his briar pipe.
'Tis then I offer silent prayer,
To thank our Lord that my man's there.

HAIL!

    Winter's passing: flowers are rising,
      Opening forth to greet the sun:
    Gloomy days will soon be over,
      Spring-time joys will have begun.

DAVID HOPE

THE FRIENDSHIP BOOK

Tuesday—January 15.

A TRAVELLER who crossed Canada on foot, all 2500 miles of it, declared that what he found most trying on his long journey was not the dangerous mountains or rivers, the forests, or dry wilderness, but the sand in his shoes. He found that the most irritating trial he had to endure.

The great trials and tragedies of life may seem the most shattering of our experiences, but somehow we find the strength to cope with them and to overcome. So often it is the little everyday irritations, worries and setbacks that get us down. A ticking clock can be more disturbing than a clap of thunder. A thoughtless word can hurt more than a blow.

It has been called the test of the trivial, and how testing it can be.

Wednesday—January 16.

WHEN the Forth Road Bridge was being planned, various types were considered. In the end it was decided to make it a suspension bridge, but would the suspension cables be strong enough? Instead of making the cables by twisting thick wire together, they made them by twisting fine wire, like thread, into thin cables, then these were twisted together like a rope to form a thick cable to last as long as the bridge itself.

It reminds me of the classical story of how men once made a great column and then were faced with the problem of hauling it into position. The women came to the rescue, each cutting off her long hair and then all weaving it into a long rope strong enough to haul the column.

As individuals our efforts may seem so small that it seems hardly worth trying. But when we all work together, with God's help, there is nothing we cannot do.

THE FRIENDSHIP BOOK

Thursday—January 17.

FEW things are more satisfying than to look back on a day and feel that we have spent it well. Marcus Cato, the great Roman statesman, soldier and writer, used to say that there were only three things in his life which he deeply regretted. The first was having revealed a secret to his wife, the second was that he had once travelled by sea when he could easily have gone by land — and the third was that he had once spent a single day without doing *anything*!

Friday—January 18.

I MET a lady in her seventies the other day and she seemed full of the joys of spring — a cheerful greeting, and a bit of conversation and she went blithely on her way. Then I came across a much younger lady, only in her late teens. She had no particular problems, as it turned out, but she was full of grumbles, a real misery. I left her with the impression that she would be old before her time, and I thought of that wise remark by Samuel Ullman: " Youth is not a time of life; it is a state of mind."

Saturday—January 19.

"A WISE man," wrote the great essayist Francis Bacon, " always makes more opportunities than he finds." It is a good thing to perform an act of kindness when somebody asks for your help—but a better thing to offer help and friendship without waiting to be asked. Isn't there someone we could give a pleasant surprise to—a phone call, a letter, a visit, a little gift, perhaps? Of course there is. So let's do it without waiting for an " opportunity " to arise !

THE FRIENDSHIP BOOK

Sunday—January 20.

Blessed is he that cometh in the name of the Lord.

Monday—January 21.

He spent his working life as an ironmonger in Fleet Street. A simple man, he loved to escape from the city to the countryside. He retired at the age of 50. Thereafter he spent much of his time sitting contentedly on the bank of a river fishing for trout with a worm.

When he was sixty he published a volume of essays under the title *The Compleat Angler*. You've heard of it? Of course. Izaak Walton's book is still widely known and widely read—the gift to posterity of the humble ironmonger who loved nature.

Tuesday—January 22.

Manchester's Albert Square and busy Deansgate are linked by John Dalton Street. Although John Dalton was not a Mancunian by birth, he lived in Manchester for fifty of his seventy-eight years, and taught mathematics and natural philosophy in the city's colleges. He is most famous for his pioneering work in atomic theory, and was the first man to invent a means of writing down chemical symbols and formulae to show how atoms combine to make molecules.

But for all his fame he was never happier than when teaching children. A visiting French scientist was once amazed to find him teaching arithmetic to a child upon his knee. And at the age of nearly 70 he continued to teach boys the elements of mathematics, counting such teaching of greater value than all his scientific discoveries.

REMEMBER . . .

Nature's beauty all around
Some take for granted, I'll be bound.
But as the years go rolling past
These are the visions we hold fast.

DAVID HOPE

THE FRIENDSHIP BOOK

Wednesday—January 23.

BURFORD in Oxfordshire is an interesting old place. It has a broad, tree-lined High Street with cool, cobbled courts leading off to intriguing old shops with bells at their doors. One afternoon I took a walk there and met a local lady who told me some interesting things about the town. I had noticed there were no street signs anywhere. When I mentioned this, she laughed. " We don't need them in Burford. Everybody knows the names. If a stranger got lost there would always be someone around to help him find the way. He would only have to ask."

It's the same in life, isn't it? Sometimes we come to a crossroads and don't know which way to go. A " Special Someone " is there, at our elbow, waiting for us to ask, ready to give the answer.

Thursday—January 24.

THE heavy iron gates standing at an entrance in Church Street, Stoke Newington, in North London, are all that is left of Abney House, the home during the first half of the eighteenth century of Sir Thomas and Lady Abney. He was a Nonconformist director of the Bank of England, and an Alderman of the City of London.

Abney House also became the home of the hymn-writer Isaac Watts. He had been invited by Sir Thomas Abney to stay with them for a spell in 1712. Many years later Isaac Watts said to Lady Abney, " I came to stay in your home for a short time—and I have been your guest for more than thirty years "

" Yes," she replied, " and we have never had a guest whose stay seemed so short."

It was the perfect tribute to the perfect guest.

THE FRIENDSHIP BOOK

Friday—January 25.

WHEN the poet Carpani asked his friend Joseph Haydn how it was that his church music was always so cheerful, the great composer replied: " I cannot make it otherwise. I write according to the thoughts I feel. When I think upon God my heart is so full of joy that the notes leap and dance, as it were, from my pen, and since God has given me a cheerful heart it will be pardoned me that I serve Him with a cheerful spirit."

Saturday—January 26.

IT was a great day when the trainees who attend the Day Centre for the Mentally Handicapped in a certain town went to the Post Office for the first time to draw their allowances. They had always received this money, but up till now it had been drawn on their behalf by the person in charge of the hostel where they lived.

Some of the money went for their keep, something into the holiday fund, and, most important, something for pocket money. Now for the very first time each trainee would have all his money in his own hand, and what a wonderful feeling of independence they had as they squared accounts for their keep and kept the pocket money to which they were entitled.

As I say, it was a great day, and some of the trainees decided a celebration was called for. So they waited till they could catch their chief instructor, Mrs Robertson, alone and announced, " We're taking you out for coffee !"

Mrs Robertson has had more expensive treats, but none that has moved her more than this gesture by handicapped men and women who wished so much to give of the little they had.

THE FRIENDSHIP BOOK

SUNDAY—JANUARY 27.

THY mercy is great above the heavens: and thy truth reacheth unto the clouds.

MONDAY—JANUARY 28.

I HOPE you, too, will get a smile from part of a conversation I couldn't help overhearing in a lift the other day.

Two bright young girls were talking about their boy friends.

One said, " I'm not going to be tied down too early. I'm not going to get married till I'm 25."

Quick as a flash, the other smilingly responded — " And I'm not going to be 25 till I'm married."

TUESDAY—JANUARY 29.

DO you ever feel that you have accomplished little, that your work has all been in vain? A friend was telling me of a Sunday school teacher he had known. A bachelor, he loved passing on the message of Christ to his pupils. But through time new methods were brought in and he felt his ways were out of date.

When he retired from his employment he went for a sea voyage, and in the course of it met a missionary returning to his mission field. The ex-teacher told him of his years in Sunday school work and ended a little sadly, " I've often wondered if I ever did any good."

The missionary smiled. " I recognised you whenever you came aboard. I was a boy in your Sunday school, and it was because of you that I am a missionary."

If we are faithful in sowing, who knows where the seed may fall?

THE FRIENDSHIP BOOK

Wednesday—January 30.

FROM the bookstall in Canterbury Cathedral came these lines :
*If nobody smiled and nobody cheered
And nobody helped us along,
If each, every minute, looked after himself
And the good things all went to the strong;
If nobody cared just a little for you,
And nobody thought about me,
And we all stood alone in the battle of life,
What a dreary old place this would be!*

Thursday—January 31.

"WHAT is the saddest case you ever knew?" I asked the matron of a hospital just retired. She thought for a minute or two and then replied, " It was a nurse I had, one of the most beautiful girls I ever saw. But she had a car accident and her face was so disfigured that she realised she would have to give up nursing—at least until she had had a long series of operations. She was engaged to be married but broke it off."

The matron shook her head, remembering. " She was so miserable and depressed I feared for her sanity." Breaking into a smile, " Then I had an idea. I took her one day to a blind children's home, and that afternoon she played with the children and for the first time I saw her look happy. Just as we were leaving, a little blind girl put her arms round her neck and said, ' I do like your voice and I know you must have a lovely face, too.' The nurse cried all the way home in the car—but it was with happiness, for she had found her life work with the blind children who came to call her ' their lovely lady'."

A sad case? Well, in a way. But what a joyful ending!

FEBRUARY

Friday—February 1.

WHAT a wonderful word "Mummy" is! Say it quietly to yourself now . . . Doesn't it make you at once think of kindness, of gentleness, of understanding and love?

A little girl once fell on the pavement in front of a woman's house and grazed her knee. She was crying, so the woman carried her into the house, bathed her knee and bandaged it up, gave her a few sweets, and then saw her safely home.

Next day the little girl knocked at the door with a lovely bunch of snowdrops, and said, "Thank you for being my mummy yesterday."

She couldn't have put it better, could she?

Saturday—February 2.

ONE of the most impressive examples of an individual who triumphed over difficulty is that of Demosthenes, the famous Greek orator who lived in the 4th century BC. His ambition was to become a successful politician, so he decided he would have to train himself to speak well in public. At first the idea seemed ridiculous. Not only were his lungs and voice weak, but he was afflicted with the most appalling stutter.

However, Demosthenes persisted. He cured his stammer by talking with pebbles in his mouth, and he strengthened his voice by going down to the sea-shore and shouting above the noise of the waves. Eventually he became not merely a good speaker, but one of the greatest who ever lived.

A splendid example of how determination can sweep aside all obstacles.

THE FRIENDSHIP BOOK

Sunday—February 3.

O LORD, how manifold are thy works! In wisdom hast thou made them all: the earth is full of thy riches.

Monday—February 4.

IN a London East End school a schoolmistress was reading to her class Shelley's *Ode To A Skylark*. In order to make sure they were understanding it she asked her pupils if they could put into different words the familiar line, " Hail to thee, blithe spirit—bird thou never wert."

An arm shot up in the back row. " Well, Robert," said the teacher, " how would you put it?"

The little Londoner piped up, " Hi, cocky! You ain't no blinkin' bird!"

Tuesday—February 5.

I AM sure that not enough emphasis is put on prayer these days.

When the soldiers in the Sudan saw the white handkerchief of General Gordon spread at the entrance to his tent they knew it was a sign that the Commander-in-Chief was not to be disturbed because he was at prayer.

Oliver Cromwell, too, always had family worship with his officers and read a chapter of the Bible before going into battle.

Abraham Lincoln used to say that he kept his mind calm and serene by spending the first ten minutes of each day in prayer.

Today many of us have lost the habit—and with it the strength to stand the strain.

The wonderful thing is that we can start again any time—tonight, today, *now*.

THE FRIENDSHIP BOOK

Wednesday—February 6.

SADHU SUNDAR SINGH, a Hindu holy man, was once travelling in the mountains with a Tibetan companion on a bitterly cold day. Both men were so nearly frozen to death that they despaired of ever reaching their destination alive.

Then they stumbled over a man half-buried in the snow, unconscious and nearly dead from exposure. Sadhu Sundar suggested that they should carry the man to shelter, but the Tibetan refused to help, declaring that it was all they could do to save themselves. So the Tibetan went on ahead whilst Sadhu Sundar, with great difficulty, got the man over his shoulder and struggled on. The extra exertion began to warm him up, and before long the man on his shoulders began to grow warm, too.

Soon they came upon the body of the Tibetan—frozen to death. While by the time Sadhu Sundar Singh reached a village the man he had rescued had recovered consciousness.

Thursday—February 7.

DURING the Second World War, when there was the danger of air raids on London, our present Queen and her sister Princess Margaret, were sent to Windsor Castle which, it was thought, would be a little safer for them. King George VI and his Queen stayed on in London. When someone suggested that the whole family should leave the country altogether to avoid any danger, the Queen (now the Queen Mother) said, " The children will not leave without me; I will not leave without the King; and the King will never leave."

The Royal couple's firm resolve to remain in London and to share the war-time dangers with their subjects endeared them to everybody.

WELCOME!

Never does our postman fail,
Rain or shine, with all the mail.
He's always welcome when he rings,
Especially when good news he brings.

DAVID HOPE

THE FRIENDSHIP BOOK

FRIDAY—FEBRUARY 8.

CAN anyone really own a mountain, or a forest or a lake?

Many years ago a President of the United States was negotiating the purchase of some land on which lived a tribe of Indians, the Suwamish.

I don't know what the President said, but the Indian chief uttered these beautiful and moving words:

" How can you buy or sell the sky—the warmth of the land? We do not own the freshness of the air or the sparkle of the water. How can you buy them from us? Every part of the earth is sacred to my people.

" Every shining pine needle, every sandy shore, every mist in the dark woods, every insect—all are holy in the experience and memory of my people.

" All things are connected. Whatever befalls the earth, befalls the sons of the earth."

SATURDAY—FEBRUARY 9.

I'M sure you've read many definitions of the difference between an optimist and a pessimist. I've just heard one of the neatest.

It's about the optimist frog and the pessimist frog who fell into a pail of milk and were in danger of being drowned. They swam around for a short time, then the pessimist gave up, sank to the bottom and was drowned.

The optimist, however, kept on till he felt he could swim no longer. And suddenly he found himself sitting on a pat of butter which he himself had churned by his swimming.

The outlook may seem hopeless, but don't give up. When things look blackest—that's the time to start swimming harder than ever!

THE FRIENDSHIP BOOK

Sunday—February 10.

As the heaven is high above the earth, so great is his mercy toward them that fear him.

Monday—February 11.

Once, many years ago, some boys were tormenting a dog and throwing stones at it, so that one of its legs was broken. Then a little girl came on the scene, went to the animal and comforted it. She bandaged the dog's leg, and before very long it had made an excellent recovery.

That dog was Florence Nightingale's very first patient.

Tuesday—February 12.

Would you think me impertinent if I suggest that you—and I—could learn a worthwhile lesson from six-year-olds?

I ask, because of a letter from Mrs Ruby Skinkle of Stayner, Ontario. It's about one of her grandchildren, Craig, who had been playing with his pal, David. As children will, they fell out. Soon they were fighting, mostly with words, until Craig's mother felt enough was enough and intervened by pointing out it was time for David to go home for his tea.

Next day Craig asked her if he could phone David and invite him over to play and stay for tea.

"I thought you two had fallen out!" she exclaimed.

"Oh, Mum," he said shaking his head, "that was *yesterday*."

Just a story about two children. Nothing in it for grown-ups?

I think there is.

THE FRIENDSHIP BOOK

Wednesday—February 13.

I WONDERED at the change in the appearance of the middle-aged woman who owns the little shop on the corner. She seemed more smart, alert and smiling in her service. She must have seen me looking my question, for she smiled as she whispered, " It's because of the mirror."

Evidently she had been worried by the increase in shop-lifting and she had placed a mirror where she could see without being seen.

" It reflected the customers in the shop," she said, " but I had to pass it ever so many times a day and I could see myself. I grew so sick of my untidy appearance that I determined to do something about it."

Sometimes it does us good to look at ourselves through other people's eyes.

Thursday—February 14.

WHAT an inspiration is Catherine Bramwell-Booth, retired Commissioner of the Salvation Army ! Now over ninety years old, still vigorous, she is as certain as ever that for all who believe in God, life is a glorious pilgrimage.

When being asked how her faith applied in modern days she stated a profound truth in very simple words :

" Men have always lived in modern days."

And it's true. In every age, whatever scientific advances may be made, we have to ask ourselves, " Am I being honest? Am I being kind? Am I being true to my faith?"

Men and women had to make these decisions when the year 100 A.D. was " modern days," and we will still have to make them when the year 2100 will be " modern days."

THE FRIENDSHIP BOOK

Friday—February 15.

EVERY morning for several years Mary Douglas has been going next door to Jack Martin's house to help him on with his left sock and shoe. You see, Jack is a widower, badly crippled with arthritis. He is marvellously independent, and somehow he manages to dress himself—all except for his left shoe and sock. So he has come to rely on Mary.

But recently Mary had to go away for a month to visit a sick relative. So day after day her husband, Archie, took over her good deed, coming in before leaving for work so that Jack would start the day properly shod.

Archie is a very busy man, much of whose spare time is spent in work as a local councillor. Some people think he is rather stern and cold. I wish they could see him as Jack Martin sees him, a busy man who yet finds time to help a neighbour in the humblest of ways.

Saturday—February 16.

WE are each of us at least three people.

There's the face we show to the lawyer. He often sees men and women at their worst.

There's the face we show to the minister. We try to let him see only our best side.

Then there's the face the doctor sees : our defences down, our fear or our courage revealed, our pretences gone.

There's perhaps not much we can do about it, but always to bear in mind the words of Robert Burns :

> *Oh, wad some power the giftie gie us*
> *To see oorsels as ithers see us,*
> *It wad frae mony a blunder free us*
> *An foolish notion.*

THE FRIENDSHIP BOOK

Sunday—February 17.

FOR with God all things are possible.

Monday—February 18.

EVERY morning Alec climbs a mountain. When I tell you it is only twenty feet high you will think that isn't much of a feat. But, you see, to get up one step Alec has to use as much energy as you and I need to walk many, many yards.

Alec is a man of forty. A few years ago he lost the power of his legs almost completely. With the aid of that godsend to the disabled called a zimmer he can get about not so badly on the level, though climbing stairs is a great trial.

At the training centre where he works he gets somebody to leave his zimmer at the top of the stairs. Then, hanging on to the railing with both hands he uses the power of his arms to pull him up step by step.

At first I found it heart-breaking to watch his efforts, but now I can only stand and admire, for he refuses to be helped.

But it's not only a matter of pride, it's also commonsense. For, as Alec explained to me, " If I depended on somebody to help me, one day there might be nobody here. Then I'd be stuck. But now I can do it on my own, even if it is a struggle, and I don't need to rely on anybody."

Isn't that a splendid kind of independence?

Tuesday—February 19.

I WROTE a letter — quite a chore,
    But I knew that it was waited for.
And what I took an hour to do,
Would pleasure give the whole day through.

THE FRIENDSHIP BOOK

WEDNESDAY—FEBRUARY 20.

THE evening service had gone well. The singing had been rousing and melodious. As the organist left the church the organ-blower said to him, " We did well tonight, didn't we?"

" What do you mean—we? *We*, indeed!" exclaimed the organist, and he stumped off.

Next Sunday morning the organist was seated at his post; he pulled out the appropriate stops and pressed his fingers on the keys. Not a sound was heard. He hurried round to the back of the organ and found the organ-blower sitting on his chair, smiling, with his arms folded. " Oh, dear," he said to the angry organist. " We're not doing so well today, are we?"

THURSDAY—FEBRUARY 21.

HOW old is old?

Our local light opera company has been making great efforts to attract younger members and they have been succeeding very well. It was delightful to see so many happy young faces in the chorus when they put on their last show.

But the leading lady didn't know where to look when she heard two of these sixteen-year-olds discussing her part.

" I think she was wonderful," said Jane.

" Oh, yes, her singing was marvellous," Margaret agreed, and then she added, " I don't know how she keeps it up—I know for a fact she was thirty-five last birthday."

The leading lady doesn't quite know how Margaret got her information about her age, but otherwise she thanks her for the compliment and hopes she'll be able to carry on singing for another year or two yet!

THE FRIENDSHIP BOOK

FRIDAY—FEBRUARY 22.

A LITTLE girl visited the dentist to have a tooth removed, and that night placed her extracted tooth under the pillow as she went to bed.

"Do you believe in fairies?" asked her mother.

"No," she replied, "but I still believe in Daddy!"

SATURDAY—FEBRUARY 23.

THE American President, Jimmy Carter, wrote his autobiography and called it *Why Not The Best?* The title stems from a gruelling interview he once had. He was asked how he had worked at the Naval Academy and if he had done his best. He thought, and then, wanting to be completely honest, he replied that he had not *always* done his best. The interviewer immediately asked, "Why not?"

When I read this I thought of another story that I had just read about 85-year-old Marevna—she likes to be called just Marevna. She now lives in Ealing, London, but was brought up in the forests of the Russian Steppes.

Marevna is a brilliant artist, and the famous Picasso was one of her closest friends; he painted her, and she painted him. When she was 83 some of her work was exhibited at a festival in Leicester. After the event this remarkable and utterly irrepressible old lady said, "I thank you young people for showing some admiration for my work, and *I hope to do better next time.*"

It's never too late to learn—especially to do one's best.

SUNDAY—FEBRUARY 24.

THE Lord is merciful and gracious, slow to anger, and plenteous in mercy.

THE FRIENDSHIP BOOK

Monday—February 25.

A VICAR was paying a few farewell calls before moving to a new parish and one elderly parishioner paid him the compliment of suggesting that his successor would not be as good as he had been.

"Oh, nonsense," he replied, flattered.

"Well," said the old lady, shaking her head, "I've lived here under five different vicars, and each new one has been worse than the last!"

Tuesday—February 26.

A FRIEND keeps these lines pinned above his desk. He is a very busy man, but he tells me that he makes sure he finds a moment to read them at least once a day:

Take time to think—*thoughts are the source of power.*

Take time to play—*play is the secret of perpetual youth.*

Take time to read—*reading is the fountain of wisdom.*

Take time to pray—*prayer can be a rock of strength in time of trouble.*

Take time to love—*loving is what makes living worthwhile.*

Take time to be friendly—*friendships give life a delicious flavour.*

Take time to laugh—*laughter is the music of the soul.*

Take time to give—*any day of the year is too short for selfishness.*

Take time to do your work well—*pride in your work nourishes the spirit.*

Take time to show appreciation—*thanks is the frosting on the cake of life.*

THE FRIENDSHIP BOOK

Wednesday—February 27.

I HEARD the other day of a Yorkshireman who went to the doctor with an injured left hand. When the doctor had dressed and bandaged it the patient asked, " Will I be able to play the violin, do you think?"

" Of course you will," replied the doctor.

" That's wonderful," replied the man with an innocent grin. " I've never been able to play it before !"

Thursday—February 28.

WHEN thirteen-year-old Carl Harvey took part in a sponsored swim at Stevenage to raise money for the British Heart Foundation, you would not have suspected that his own heart was fitted with a pace-maker — as is also that of his sister. He is so grateful to be able to lead a normal life that he has already made up his mind to be a heart surgeon.

So often we find that the keenest workers for charity are those who have something to be really thankful for. If only we all counted our blessings, what a lot of good reasons we would find for helping others!

Friday—February 29.

LITTLE Robert, who for a long time had been wanting a baby sister, was saying his prayers. He had been told that if he prayed very hard a baby might arrive.

Robert was only six, but he had lived observantly, and one night, after saying his prayer for a little sister, he added, " And, dear Jesus, if you haven't got her quite finished, don't wait to put in her tonsils 'cause they just have to be cut out anyway !"

OLD TIME

*An ancient heritage is ours
Where, under tall cathedral towers,
Along the narrow streets we go
—No need to hurry, take it slow.
Here in these old and mellow ways,
Lucky the folk who spend their days.*

DAVID HOPE

MARCH

SATURDAY—MARCH 1.

*WHEN a good friend walks beside us
  On the road that we must keep,
Our burdens seem less heavy
  And the hills are not so steep.
The weariest miles pass swiftly,
  Taken in a joyous stride,
And all the world seems brighter
  When a friend walks by your side.*

SUNDAY—MARCH 2.

HE that believeth on me hath everlasting life.

MONDAY—MARCH 3.

MARGARET BLAIN was on her way to a paper shop in Cathcart Road, in Glasgow, when she noticed that the woman coming towards her was blind. Hearing Margaret's step the woman asked if she would help her across the road. Of course, Margaret was happy to do so. On the way over, the woman mentioned how much she was looking forward to summer, for then she can feel the sun's brightness.

Crossing back on to her own side, Margaret noticed the grounds of the church she had just passed were a mass of colour. Not just the yellow daffodils, but the green of the grass, and the dark richness of the shrubs with their glossy leaves. Yet she hadn't really noticed them a minute earlier. As she went on her way to the paper shop she looked around her with a new awareness and appreciation.

Never again, she decided, would she take the gift of sight for granted.

THE FRIENDSHIP BOOK

Tuesday—March 4.

CHRISTIAN Aid has continued the history of mission by providing the resources and the implements so that underdeveloped countries can help themselves. The organisation is a comparatively new one, but its aims and methods are not so different from those of the first missionaries.

One of the early missionaries in Central Africa discovered that most of the tribes worshipped the sun. After a long drought they gathered together to pray for rain to the sun god. " Why don't you pray to your Christian God?" they challenged the missionary. " See if He will send you rain."

Instead of kneeling down to pray as they expected him to, the missionary began to dig where he knew there would be underground springs. They were surprised when water appeared — but not impressed. " That water comes not from heaven but from the earth," they said.

" And that is the lesson I would teach you," said the missionary. " To work is to pray."

Wednesday—March 5.

VIOLETS, with their sweet perfume, are among the most beloved of flowers. But have you ever wondered, as you held a posy of violets in your hand, why the fragrance seems to be so fleeting?

A friend, who is a botanist, has been telling me the secret. The violet contains a substance known as ionine which dulls the sense of smell. So it is not the flower that loses its perfume but our noses that lose their ability to appreciate it. The perfume is there constantly in all its charm.

Isn't it the same with many of life's blessings? They are there all around us—but, sadly, it's only now and again that we notice and appreciate them.

THE FRIENDSHIP BOOK

Thursday—March 6.

MOST of us have felt at times we'd do almost anything to get our own back for a wounding word or a cruel action. A friend who spent part of his last holiday in a small village in France was telling me a wonderful story of how one man faced up to the problem of revenge.

He was a Frenchman, a very active member of the Resistance movement. One day the Germans burst into his house and for the rest of the war he hung on to life in a concentration camp. He had been betrayed by somebody in the village.

When he returned home after the war he was just a shadow of the strong man he had been. A neighbour said to him, " Now you're back you'll be able to look for the man who gave you away and then you'll get your own back."

To his amazement, the man who had been so terribly wronged replied quietly, " I know who told the Germans. But revenge? What would be the use? Would it make me any happier?"

Only a man with a great spirit could see things in this light, but who can doubt that he was right?

Friday—March 7.

LET'S share a story with a smile from an old friend of mine, Jack McKibbin, of Dundonald, Belfast.

It seems an elderly woman was having a TV installed, a gift from her family. The TV man showed her how it worked, how to plug it in, switch it on, &c.

" Are you sure I won't get a shock?" she asked nervously.

" Not till you see the programmes!" he answered with a grin.

THE FRIENDSHIP BOOK

Saturday—March 8.

I SUPPOSE you've heard the story of the famous judge who spoke rudely to his partner during a game of whist. When called on to apologise, he muttered, " Sorry, but I thought for the moment I was speaking to my wife."

Well, that's just a story, of course, but there's more than a grain of truth in it. Life in some families would be a lot happier if all members treated each other with the consideration they show to outsiders. In the words of the poet :

*We have careful thought for the stranger
And a smile for the welcome guest,
But we vex our own by word and tone
Though we love our own the best.*

Sunday—March 9.

BLESS the Lord, O my soul, and forget not all his benefits.

Monday—March 10.

MIRIAM EKER, of Longsight, Manchester, sent me these lines :

*There's joy in going an errand,
In walking along the street,
In having a word of greeting,
For the people that I meet.
There's joy in using a duster,
In keeping the doorstep clean,
In fixing on my windows
Bright curtains to be seen.
There's joy in doing the washing,
In cooking, and sweeping the floor
And I thank thee, Lord, for the blessing
Of health to do each chore.*

THE FRIENDSHIP BOOK

TUESDAY—MARCH 11.

A BIT of example can be worth more than a volume of preaching.

I've been thinking of a visit the Lady of the House and I made the other day. It was to a woman who used to be a childhood friend and whom she hadn't seen for many years.

While we were sitting enjoying a cup of tea there came two knocks at the door. First a little girl came to show " Aunt Janet " her latest drawing. Then a little boy brought along a new kitten.

Janet welcomed the children as though she hadn't seen them for years and sent them each away happy with a sweet.

" You're very good with them," said the Lady of the House. " Not everybody would have your patience."

Janet smiled. " Do you know who taught me to do this? It was your mother, when we used to be neighbours. No child ever left her house without a smile and a kiss. It's something I've never forgotten."

As I said, it's wonderful the effect a good example can have on a person's life.

WEDNESDAY—MARCH 12.

DR MICHELE CLEMENTS is a much-respected specialist in babies' hearing at the City of London Maternity Hospital.

Once she was asked to talk on radio and TV about her work. Next day, to her surprise, two army officers drew up in a car and delivered to Dr Clements half of baby Peter Phillips' christening cake.

It was a touching gesture from Princess Anne to a doctor whom she had never even met.

THE FRIENDSHIP BOOK

Thursday—March 13.

I DO not know who wrote these words, but it seems to me that the writer says in a few words a truth that is escaping many people today in their endless striving for what they consider "the good life."

The glory of life
Is to love, not to be loved;
To serve, not to be served;
To be a strong hand in the dark
To another in the time of need;
To be a cup of strength to any soul
In a crisis of weakness.
That is to know the glory of life.

Friday—March 14.

SOMETIMES it is as blessed to receive as to give—and more difficult. I'm thinking of Robbie and Mary, new neighbours of ours, though, as you guess, I'm not giving you their right names.

Robbie is more or less housebound and quite often ill. This makes it difficult for Mary to get out to the shops so the Lady of the House decided she would help Mary by offering to bring in anything she needed.

And Mary was very grateful. Too grateful, in fact. For every time the Lady of the House did a small service, Mary would reward this with a small gift.

Both the Lady of the House and I know that Mary means well. But good neighbours don't look for rewards, and, I'm sorry to say, the Lady of the House has become so embarrassed that she's almost unwilling to offer to do Mary a good turn.

Which is a pity, because they both have such good intentions.

THE FRIENDSHIP BOOK

SATURDAY—MARCH 15.

WHEN asked by their cookery teacher why their oven was set at 400 when all the others were at 200, two small sisters immediately replied, " Well, miss, there's two of us using it!"

SUNDAY—MARCH 16.

IF any man serve me, him will my Father honour.

MONDAY—MARCH 17.

WHAT a joy it was for Mrs MacIntosh of Glasgow when she learned about the Mother's Day present that was coming to her! House-bound and living three floors up, she was cut off from all her friends, so the telephone that her brothers and sons were going to put in for her would open up a whole new world.

But that wasn't all. The Post Office had arranged for six of the people having a phone installed on Mother's Day to receive a beautiful bouquet. Mrs MacIntosh was one of the lucky six. When the bouquet was delivered to her door she was one of the happiest women in Glasgow.

And I haven't told you yet about the engineer who put in the phone. He was working overtime on a Saturday morning. That is the one day in the week Mrs MacIntosh's home help does not come. After he had connected up the phone and seen that it was working he noticed her lighting the fire and putting the ashes aside till her home help came next day.

Gallant man that he was, he picked up the bucket, and carried it down two flights of stairs, leaving Mrs MacIntosh feeling that there is still far more kindness and helpfulness in the world than most people imagine!

BANG! BANG!

> We're in the band, the envy of
> The other girls and boys.
> We like it best when we can make
> A really LOVELY noise!

DAVID HOPE

THE FRIENDSHIP BOOK

Tuesday—March 18.

IF you have ever been to Bourton-on-the-Water in the Cotswolds, with the river spanned by several small bridges running down its main street, you will probably have seen or visited " Birdland."

" Birdland " is an open-air aviary inhabited by colourful and exotic birds. It is owned by Len Hills, and is open to the public. One cold winter morning Len saw a lady standing in the entrance shivering in the cold. He invited her into his home for warmth and refreshment, and learned that she was waiting for her son who was a spastic, and that they came regularly to " Birdland " so that he could paint the birds.

Len met the spastic artist, saw his work, and, thanks to his generosity, Paul Nicholas now exhibits and sells his work at Bourton-on-the-Water.

Now, whenever I hear of Bourton-on-the-Water I do not think of the picturesque bridges across a sparkling river, but of a bridge that was built by a big-hearted man to cross a gap in another man's life.

Wednesday—March 19.

DURING the Crimean War, when British soldiers were performing many brave deeds in battle, Queen Victoria urged that a suitable commemorative medal be issued as an award for acts of outstanding gallantry in action.

When the design of the award was completed, the Queen wrote to the Secretary of State for War recommending an alteration to the suggested inscription which then read, " For the Brave."

Her Majesty requested that the inscription should be altered to " For Valour." And so was born the Victoria Cross, the highest decoration for bravery that can be awarded.

THE FRIENDSHIP BOOK

Thursday—March 20.

AT 3 Kent Street, Tokoroa, New Zealand, lives a cheerful friend of ours called Agnes Innes.

Now and again she sends us a newsy airmail from the other side of the world. As she tells me about life there, she often drops in a simple but profound thought. Let me share this one with you:

I often remind myself never to spend too long looking at those with more than myself, but to cast a glance, instead, at those with less.

Friday—March 21.

YOU might not expect to find a sermon in a jigsaw puzzle, but you could be wrong.

John had dropped in on his friend Jeff and found him very much down in the dumps. Life, Jeff felt, was passing him by. Things weren't going well at work. He was snappy and arguing about small things with his family. Feeling sorry for himself, in fact, and a bit of a failure.

John tried to convince him it was just a phase, but he was hard to cheer. Then John had a flash of inspiration when he saw a nearly completed jigsaw on the table.

He picked up a piece, asking, "Jeff, would it matter to the final picture if this small piece were missing?"

"Of course," Jeff frowned. "What on earth do you mean?" Then he grinned.

I'm sure you've realised why!

At work, at home, in your street or wherever—you are a part, no matter how humble, in life's jigsaw. Some picture wouldn't be complete without *you*.

When you're feeling low, it might help to remember that.

THE FRIENDSHIP BOOK

S̲a̲t̲u̲r̲d̲a̲y̲—M̲a̲r̲c̲h̲ 2̲2̲.

PASSING a cinema one morning in the rush hour, I was startled out of my reverie when a woman sweeping out the foyer suddenly dropped her brush with a clatter and rushed off along the pavement.

Next moment she was leading a blind lady round a roadsweeper's barrow sitting in her path. Like me, lots of other folk were passing, but only the cleaning lady had spotted the danger and prevented what could have been a nasty accident.

Opportunities to help others are always around us, but how many we must miss! Thank goodness for people like that Mrs Mop who spot danger for others before it strikes—and act quickly to avert it.

S̲u̲n̲d̲a̲y̲—M̲a̲r̲c̲h̲ 2̲3̲.

AND ye shall know the truth, and the truth shall make you free.

M̲o̲n̲d̲a̲y̲—M̲a̲r̲c̲h̲ 2̲4̲.

A MINISTER'S son was asked how he liked his father's sermon that Sunday. "Fine," he replied, "but there were three places where he could have stopped."

Mark Twain, the famous American writer and humourist, would have agreed with him. He went to hear a famous preacher and confessed, " He was so brilliant to begin with that I determined to give all I had to the collection plate, but the longer he went on I calculated how much less I could give, and when at last he stopped I borrowed something out of the plate to pay my bus fare home."

Any housewife will tell you that even the best of cakes can be spoiled by overcooking!

D

THE FRIENDSHIP BOOK

TUESDAY—MARCH 25.

I HAD been invited to attend a marvellous "Fiddlers' Rally" in the wee Scottish town of Kirriemuir. Men and women, boys and girls, played jigs and hornpipes and haunting slow airs on their fiddles, and Mr Calder, the adjudicator, commented on the performances with wit and charm.

He told us he was very fond of the double bass. When he was a student, waiting to join the music society, the conductor had looked at him and said, "You'll play the double bass."

So Mr Calder played the double bass, and grew to love it. And when his sons grew up, one of them followed his example and played the double bass while the other took up the cello. Now they both play in famous orchestras, one with the London Philharmonic and the other with the Halle.

"And to think," smiled Mr Calder, "all this happened because the conductor simply said to me, 'You'll play the double bass.'"

Of course, as Mr Calder knows better than anybody, that isn't the whole story. There must be a willingness to take our opportunities. But isn't it true that our lives are often shaped by something that at the time seems quite trivial, but years after we recognise as having been a turning point?

WEDNESDAY—MARCH 26.

THE rain was pouring down and the wind was howling, but the old gentlemen in the eventide home were warm and comfortable. A lady visitor, seeking to be polite, said as she passed by, "Terrible day! Do you think it's going to improve?"

To which came the reply, "Well, it always has done, hasn't it?"

Wasn't that just the perfect answer!

THE FRIENDSHIP BOOK

Thursday—March 27.

ROBERT STROUD spent more than forty years in Alcatraz Prison, and probably saved his sanity by becoming an authority on birds. He was known as "The Birdman of Alcatraz."

A girl of 22 once wrote to him. She had lost a leg by amputation, had undergone several surgical operations, and felt life wasn't worth living. When she read the story of Robert Stroud it gave her renewed hope.

In his reply to her, "The Birdman" wrote: "Neither of us can afford to know the meaning of the word 'can't'; I am sending you a canary who will tell you that over and over."

It did so, and thanks to the bird's cheerful encouragement the girl rapidly improved in both health and outlook on life.

Friday—March 28.

DR WALKER was sitting in his office in a Galilean hospital where he worked for nineteen years when he was told that someone wanted to see him. The man's name meant nothing to him, and the young man appeared rather shy, but eventually he got to the point of his visit, "Do you remember treating a young Jew paralysed from the waist downwards and tending him for many months?"

"I do indeed," replied Dr Walker.

"Well," replied his visitor, "that was me. When I heard you were still here I just wanted to come and thank you."

The wonderful thing about this story is that it was seventeen years since the man had been Dr Walker's patient. This was the first chance he had had to thank him and he was not going to let it pass by. It's never too late . . .

THE FRIENDSHIP BOOK

Saturday—March 29.

THERE is a pleasant little story told about the late Albert Einstein, the great physicist, a man of immense intellect, with a world-wide reputation. The closing years of his life he spent in America, working in New York and living in Princeton, New Jersey. One evening when he got off the train at the railway station in Princeton he was met by a boy who had been waiting some time for him. The boy approached the great man diffidently and asked him if he would explain a problem in mathematics which he had to solve for a school exercise. The professor, though he may well have been tired after a busy day's work, smiled and said he would try. So there in that station, amid the throng of travellers, the most renowned physicist in the world took time to help a young boy with his homework.

Sunday—March 30.

FOR the Lord is good; his mercy is everlasting; and his truth endureth to all generations.

Monday—March 31.

JOHN WESLEY told once how he had been walking in St Paul's churchyard when he had observed two women. One was talking and gesticulating violently, while the other stood perfectly still and silent. Just as Wesley came up to them the noisy one stamped her foot at her imperturbable neighbour, exclaiming, " Speak, so that I may have something to say."

Wesley said afterwards, " That was a lesson to me. I learned that day that silence is often the best answer to abuse."

APRIL

Tuesday—April 1.

IN the days when parsons often had large families, there was one tribe of daughters of the vicarage who were all so obviously happy that a friend asked their father if he had taught them some secret.

He replied: "When anything upsets them I ask them to sing. If I hear them criticising anyone I suggest that they sing. They sing away all causes of discontent and disturbance."

He would have approved of that lilting chorus:
Sing when the day is bright,
Sing through the darkest night,
Every day,
All the way,
Let us sing—sing—sing!

Wednesday—April 2.

WE have scientists who can land men on the moon, but there are still many apparently simple questions that no one has succeeded in answering.

Henry Douglas-Home, who, as the bird expert of the BBC, made so many friends, tells in a delightful book of receiving a letter from a little girl who had listened to him giving a talk on the cuckoo.

"How is it," she asked, "that the cuckoo, who has never seen its parents, can grow up to say, 'Cuckoo-cuckoo'? If the stork dropped a British baby in China it wouldn't grow up speaking English, would it?"

"An unanswerable question," said Henry Douglas-Home. We don't know everything yet!

TRUST

My mistress wasn't going far
  She told me as she said good-bye;
She didn't even lock the car—
  That's rather strange. I wonder why?

DAVID HOPE

THE FRIENDSHIP BOOK

Thursday—April 3.

EVERY housewife knows that there's no use just cleaning the outsides of cups and pots and pans—if you haven't cleaned the insides as well, the washing-up's not properly done.

Isn't there a message here for us? I'm thinking, as I write, of a churchgoer I know. She's a regular attender, and, to all outward appearances, a good Christian. But talk to her and you find she has very little sympathy for others not as lucky as herself, and some of the things she says about people are—well, not very pleasant.

She would do well to reflect on the parable of the pots and pans.

Friday—April 4.

THE number of people in the world today who opt out of society and become homeless wanderers, seems to be growing. Occasionally, however, I am pleased to say you hear of one picking up the threads of life once more.

The man I am thinking of used to visit the Salvation Army Centre in Anderston, Glasgow. Shabby and unkempt in appearance, he came regularly to their soup kitchen, leaving as silently as he had arrived. The staff tried to talk to him to bring him out of his shell, but to no avail. Then, going through some clothes which had been handed in, they came across a nice silk tie and decided to offer it to him. He took it gratefully, and the next day when he came his beard was neatly trimmed and he was wearing his new tie.

I'm told that from that day on he never looked back. Eventually he got a job and moved into digs.

Life had begun for him once more—thanks to the gift of a second-hand tie.

THE FRIENDSHIP BOOK

Saturday—April 5.

A ROMANIAN member of the Greek Orthodox Church was describing the ancient custom of waiting for Easter. The congregation sits in a darkened church until the priest announces the Resurrection of Jesus by lighting a candle. The priest then takes it outside so that others may light their candles from its flame, thus spreading the light of Christ from person to person.

I had heard about this custom before, but what caught my attention was the speaker's comment: "You can receive the light from any other person . . . And in the same way we learn the truth from other people, no matter who they are. The young can learn from the old, the old can learn from the young . . . it is all the same."

Sunday—April 6.

THEN the same day at evening, came Jesus and stood in the midst, and saith unto them, Peace be unto you.

Monday—April 7.

THE bus was crowded and I got up to offer a lady my seat. She smiled and thanked me.

Minutes later a much older lady, clutching a heavy message basket, struggled on to the bus. She was obviously having difficulty and I saw the younger lady rise to her feet and offer the seat that had been "my" seat, to the newcomer.

Down the crowded bus my eyes met those of "my" lady. We smiled to each other. We had never met before and probably would never meet again. But for a moment we were partners in a good deed.

THE FRIENDSHIP BOOK

Tuesday—April 8.

WHAT'S the first thing you think of when you wake up in the morning? The day's work? Paying bills? A visit to the dentist?

None of these can be avoided. But how much better a frame of mind we would all be in to face these problems if we were to start the day like the philosopher Emerson, who wrote:

"I awoke this morning with devout thanksgiving for my friends—the old and the new."

Could there be a better way to begin today—or any day?

Wednesday—April 9.

I MET my friend Mary in the market-place. She went through a bad patch when her husband John was made redundant. With their family they had to leave their neat little home in town and move to an isolated cottage when John found a new job.

"How are you liking your new home?" I asked.

"I love it," smiled Mary. "The first day I was feeling low and ready to weep. Then my little girl came in from the field outside carrying a bunch of cuckoo flowers—lady-smocks, I used to call them. 'Look, Mum,' she said, 'aren't we lucky to be here in a house surrounded by flowers!'

"Suddenly I realised," said Mary, "that I was still surrounded by all that I love best in the world—a good, kind husband who was well and strong, and our children. I suddenly saw our new home, not as second-best, but as a new beginning. Things seemed to go right from that moment—I don't know why."

I know why—and between you and me, I think Mary does, too.

THE FRIENDSHIP BOOK

Thursday—April 10.

THERE'S an old Yorkshire story about a farmer who had a very mischievous brownie living on his farm. It wreaked havoc for many years, curdling the milk, spoiling the butter and scaring everybody by throwing things about the house.

At last the farmer had had enough. He would move house and get away from the brownie. He piled all his furniture on to a cart, sat his wife and son on top, tied the cow behind, and set off to find a new home.

He had travelled quite a long way when he glanced down. There, beside him on the seat, was the brownie. The poor farmer turned the horse round and went home again.

Running away from a problem never solves it, does it?

Friday—April 11.

MANY years ago a group of notable men were discussing short prayers. Sir William Wyndham said that the shortest prayer he had ever heard was that of a soldier before the Battle of Blenheim:

"Oh, God, if there be a God, save my soul, if I have a soul."

The Bishop of Rochester said quietly, "Sir William, your prayer is indeed very short, but I remember another almost as short, but much better, offered up likewise by a poor soldier in the same circumstances:

"'Oh God, if, in the day of battle I forget Thee, do not Thou forget me.'"

The members of the august company who had been ready to laugh at Sir William's prayer, were hushed to silence.

THE FRIENDSHIP BOOK

Saturday—April 12.

BENJAMIN BARBER of Bradwell, in the Derbyshire Peak District, when interviewed for a job as a mining agent, was asked what religion he professed.

He replied, " A Methodist, sir," and the mine proprietor said, " Well, if I engage you I shall expect you to renounce all connections with the Methodists and attend the Church of England."

" Sir," said Benjamin, " I am a poor man, and I have a large family; but rather than renounce the Methodists I will beg my bread from door to door."

The mine proprietor recognised a man of principle. Benjamin got the job and was ever afterwards referred to as " my trusty servant Benjamin."

This story is told by Benjamin's great-great-great-grandson, the former Conservative Chancellor of the Exchequer, Mr Anthony Barber, who is rightly proud of his much respected ancestor.

Sunday—April 13.

THEN he arose, and rebuked the wind and the raging of the water: and they ceased, and there was a calm.

Monday—April 14.

GRANDFATHER JONES was quite deaf. Although he could not hear the sermon he still went to church every Sunday.

" Why do you bother going when you cannot hear what is going on?" asked one of his grandchildren.

Grandfather considered for a moment and then he said, " I want everyone to know whose side I am on."

THE LESSON

Let me not make myself a fort
  Where friendship may not enter,
But give me friends of every sort,
  My home for them a centre.
Castles with their walls so stout
Were built, you see, to keep folk out.

DAVID HOPE

THE FRIENDSHIP BOOK

Tuesday—April 15.

THIS is a story that my little friend Philippa never tires of.

There was once a beautiful and wise queen who lived in Persia. One day a nobleman from a nearby country came to visit her and she showed him round her wonderful palace with all its fabulous treasures. There were caskets of silver and of gold, diamonds, pearls and rubies and other precious stones. There were lovely gardens filled with exquisitely perfumed flowers, stables full of fine horses, and all manner of marvellous things.

The nobleman was amazed.

" And which do you count your most precious treasures?" he ventured to ask.

" Come with me," smiled the queen. She opened a golden door and there, lying asleep, were her children, a little girl and boy.

" These are my most precious treasures," said the queen.

A wise queen indeed.

Wednesday—April 16.

MRS GEORGINA HALL, of Oldham, has some lovely memories. One day she sat down, wrote a few lines of verse about them and posted them to me. She calls her verse " Silver and Gold."

I have so many memories of so many things, of golden days flying on silver heeled wings; of hours in the meadow with daisy-crowned hair; wild berries in hedgerows we so loved to share; warm feet in cool water that ran over stones; smoke fires of autumn, pine needles and cones; moonlight and starlight, a nightingale's song, the lace web of spiders, deceptively strong. Thank God for the past, and the present that sings of every-day pleasures that just living brings.

THE FRIENDSHIP BOOK

Thursday—April 17.

ISN'T it strange how smoothly life runs for everyone but ourselves? *Their* tasks never seem to be as difficult and as wearying as our own. The grass is always greener on the other side of the fence.

I am thinking, as I write, of two young mothers who live farther down the road. I stopped to watch them working hard in their gardens one fine day, attacking the weeds with fervour and doing a really good job. I expressed my admiration of their work to one of them.

"But this is not my garden," she smiled. "I never did like gardening, and neither did my friend Mary next door. So we changed places. I weed her garden one afternoon a week and she goes round and does mine. That way we both feel that we are working for someone else and we get on with the job. Afterwards we have a cup of tea together, and it's lovely to go back home and see all the work done. And do you know, we really enjoy gardening now!"

It seems that not only is the grass greener on the other side of the fence but it's easier to cut, too!

Friday—April 18.

THE English painter, Sir Frank Dicksee, did a picture which he called "The Two Crowns." It depicts a young Roman conqueror riding up the Appian Way with a golden crown on his head and hailed by the cheering crowds.

As he rides he passes a shrine by the roadside in which is set a figure of the Christ with the crown of thorns on his head. And as the Roman victor passes he looks into the eyes of the crucified one with a wistful look as if he were realising that the other has won a greater victory and achieved greater glory than he could ever attain.

THE FRIENDSHIP BOOK

Saturday—April 19.

Professor Gossip, one of the foremost preachers of a past generation, often told how one night, while a minister in Glasgow, he felt exhausted after an evening of visiting and hesitated while he contemplated climbing stairs yet again to make the last call on his list. While he hesitated he was conscious of someone brushing past him as if an unseen presence was mounting the stairs. The experience was so vivid that Dr Gossip, with renewed strength, followed up the stair to make his call.

In a state of almost sheer exhaustion, Scott, the explorer, with two companions, returned to their tent at the South Pole and, as they rested, Scott turned to his two companions and said, " Did you not feel there was a fourth person walking with us on the way?" The others agreed.

That unseen presence has walked with many, encouraging them to carry on in difficult times.

Sunday—April 20.

For a good tree bringeth not forth corrupt fruit; neither doth a corrupt tree bring forth good fruit.

Monday—April 21.

Some time ago an elderly gentleman came across a small boy crying, and asked what the matter was.

" Jimmy Green hit me," sobbed the little chap.

" Tut, tut!" said the elderly gentleman. " Why didn't you hit him back?"

" Because then it would be his turn again!" wailed the boy.

THE FRIENDSHIP BOOK

Tuesday—April 22.

A HOUSEWIFE in New Jersey was looking forward to watching the evangelist Dr Billy Graham on television. About an hour before the programme was due to start she switched on her set. Nothing happened. No sound, no picture—nothing! She telephoned the repair man at once, but as it was Sunday he said he could not come until Monday morning; he did not work on Sundays.

Just before the housewife replaced the receiver she sighed and said, "Oh, why did this have to happen—I had set my heart on hearing Billy Graham."

Within ten minutes there was a knock at her door. It was the repair man. He told her he, too, had been looking forward to watching Billy Graham and he could understand how disappointed she was at the prospect of having to miss him. He mended the set, and then they both sat down and enjoyed the programme together.

Wednesday—April 23.

A RICH man engaged an artist to execute a piece of sculpture for him. Some weeks later, having been away on business, it seemed to him that the artist had made little progress. "What have you been doing?" asked the employer angrily.

"Working on the figure."

"But I see nothing done since my last visit."

"Well," replied the artist, "I have brought out this muscle, I have modified this part of the dress and I have slightly changed the expression of the lip."

"But these are trifles!" said the man.

"True, sir," said the artist quietly. "But perfection is made up of trifles."

COMPLETE

    The beauty of a peaceful lake
        Can never charm us quite so much
    As when a happy family
        Provides the final magic touch.

                              DAVID HOPE

THE FRIENDSHIP BOOK

Thursday—April 24.

JIM ANDERSON of Edinburgh was, for a time, in the Royal Infirmary there.

One of the other patients in the ward, old Davie, was making slow progress after his operation. No amount of reassurance from the doctors or the ward sister seemed to make any difference. When Jim and the other patients tried to cheer him up they got the impression that the old shepherd would rather be left alone.

Until—one morning they noticed something. After helping to make his bed and propping him up, one of the young nurses gave old Davie a wee kiss and a cuddle before she left! Of course, word soon got round the ward—and next morning all the men were sitting up in bed smiling, while to a chorus of whistles and envious catcalls, they watched Davie " take his medicine."

Of course, it was all in good part. After that, Davie never seemed to look back. When the day came for him to return to his flocks on the bonnie Border hills he walked smartly down the ward, his wife on one arm, and his new sweetheart on the other!

It was not found necessary to administer the " kiss of life " to any of the other patients. The nurses declared none of them were half as handsome as Davie!

Friday—April 25.

ABOUT sixty years ago a nervous little man was on his way to see the Dean of Lincoln. He saw the Dean's gardener, and, tongue-tied, asked, " Is the Bean dizzy?"

Without turning a hair the gardener looked up at him and, smiling, replied, " Yes, he's over there—boiling his icicle."

THE FRIENDSHIP BOOK

Saturday—April 26.

Mr THOMAS ARNOLD, headmaster of Rugby School from 1828 to 1842, aimed to produce " First, religious and moral principle; secondly, gentlemanly conduct; and, thirdly, intellectual ability."

One day early in his career he lost his temper with one of his less bright pupils. The boy said to him, " Why do you speak angrily, sir? I *am* doing the best I can."

Years afterwards Dr Arnold said, " I never felt so ashamed in my life. I have never forgotten that boy's rebuke."

From then on he always treated his pupils as reasoning and reasonable human beings, so that when he died in 1842 he was widely regarded as probably the greatest headmaster in the country.

Sunday—April 27.

For thy mercy is great unto the heavens, and thy truth unto the clouds.

Monday—April 28.

Tom was an old London tramp. Every day at twelve o'clock he would go into a church, walk down the aisle and kneel in front of the altar. He had a very simple prayer : " Jesus, this is Tom; Jesus, this is Tom."

Then Tom had an accident and had to go into hospital. After a few days the nurses noticed that every day at twelve o'clock he liked to be left on his own for a few minutes. When they asked him why, he replied in a quiet whisper, " A friend comes to the end of my bed and says, ' Tom, this is Jesus; Tom, this is Jesus.' "

THE FRIENDSHIP BOOK

Tuesday—April 29.

IT was a shattering blow for Andrew Fairgrieve when the surgeon told him that what he had thought was gout in his foot was something more serious and his leg would have to be amputated below the knee.

For, though Andrew is in his late fifties, you would have had to go far to find a fitter man. He worked hard and played hard. For a day after receiving his bad news he scarcely spoke a word. Then, his wife told me, it was as though, overnight, he had come to a great decision and he became his usual cheerful self.

He chatted and joked with the surgeon the day before his operation. Afterwards he kept the ward in constant good humour with jokes against himself.

At the hospital to which he was sent for the fitting of an artificial leg he amazed the staff by the determination he showed in getting about on his new limb. He was out a fortnight before the surgeon thought possible.

I tell this story because Andrew, by his courage, gave strength to all those around him. It was his wife who paid him this tribute: " He seemed to be sorry for everybody in the ward, but he was never sorry for himself."

Wednesday—April 30.

WHEN the sun is setting
  And we watch its dying ray,
We never doubt it will appear
To light another day.
So let us face OUR future,
  Secure in faith that He
Who rules sunrise and sunset,
  Keeps watch o'er you and me.

THE WAY AHEAD

*The road of life's not always smooth —
Of course, there will be rain;
But step out briskly, and the sun
Will soon shine down again.*

DAVID HOPE

MAY

Thursday—May 1.

*NO man or woman you may know
    Has reached perfection yet,
And that is true of me AND you—
    A point not to forget.
If you look for another's faults,
    You're sure to find a few;
But if you seek their virtues, why,
    You're sure to find them, too!
Expect the best from folk you meet—
    It helps to keep life rich and sweet.*

Friday—May 2.

ON May 2, 1519, there died one of the servants of the King of France. Did I say one? Perhaps I should have said eight—for he was a painter who painted world-famous pictures ; a sculptor whose services were coveted by princes and statesmen ; a poet and a musician ; a designer of mechanical toys which caused much good fun in the courts of royalty ; an engineer upon whose skill some of the foremost captains of his day depended ; a scientist who held views of astronomy far beyond those of many of his contemporaries ; and a philosopher with a true understanding of human nature.

Leonardo da Vinci has been described as possibly the most diversely gifted man who has ever lived. For him the world was crowded with secrets about which he was curious to the end.

But perhaps he is best known for his painting of the *Mona Lisa,* a portrait painted with soft music played in the background throughout the sitting in order to keep a smile on the face of the sitter.

THE FRIENDSHIP BOOK

SATURDAY—MAY 3.

I KNOW a woman everybody simply calls Auntie Anne. If anyone is in trouble, Auntie Anne is there lending a hand. It may be minding a baby, running a few errands, or simply making a cup of tea and staying for a chat.

"A bit of help's worth a lot of pity," she always says with a smile. Auntie Anne has sayings for every occasion. Once, one of her nieces protested that she would never be able to repay her for all she had done. Auntie Anne retorted, "Tush! Whoever heard of a kitten giving milk to a cat?"

SUNDAY—MAY 4.

CAST thy burden upon the Lord, and he shall sustain thee.

MONDAY—MAY 5.

WHEN Group Captain Peter Townsend, after a brilliant career as a fighter pilot, was appointed an equerry at Buckingham Palace, he met Sir Winston Churchill on many occasions. In the story of his life entitled *Time and Chance* he tells of a valuable lesson he learned at one of these meetings.

He was waiting to take the Prime Minister in to the King and through habit he tapped the barometer. "I'm afraid the glass is going down, sir," he said to Sir Winston.

"Why are you *afraid*?" the great man demanded.

Townsend muttered something about the weather being unsuitable for our fighter aircraft.

As it turned out he was right, but never again, he said, did he use that defeatist expression "I'm afraid."

COLOURS

> Summer with her ample brush
>   Paints the countryside:
> Some red, some blue, a lot of green
>   Scattered far and wide.

*And there are certain favoured spots
She most displays her skills,
For lucky folk whose homes lie hid
In hollows 'neath the hills.*

DAVID HOPE

THE FRIENDSHIP BOOK

Tuesday—May 6.

WHAT are the gifts you would most wish to pass on to a daughter? The wisdom of Solomon, perhaps? Understanding? Compassion?

Early in the 19th century the then Duchess of Kent gave three gifts to her newly-born daughter—duty, simplicity—and the name Victoria. Duty showed in a reign of nearly sixty-four devoted years. Simplicity was evident in the Queen's delight in small, ordinary things. Whilst there will never be another who elevates the name Victoria to such a high level.

Wednesday—May 7.

IN the Renfield Church Centre, Glasgow, hangs a magnificent tapestry of the Last Supper.

To know how it comes to be there you have to go back to Berlin before the war. There a young German girl has a boy friend who is a Jew. For that reason alone she is taken to a police station to be questioned. She leaves Berlin and tries to make a new life in Czechoslovakia. But soon the Nazis move in there, too, and she moves again—to Britain. Here she marries an Austrian. Then war breaks out.

What, she wonders, will happen to her? Friends and neighbours go to the forces. Clydebank is blitzed, but in Garnethill she meets only sympathy and understanding. Gradually her fears disappear and she and her husband settle down. Today Mrs Mary Adler still lives in Glasgow. She made the tapestry I mentioned and handed it over to the people of Garnethill as a humble and unassuming token of her everlasting gratitude to the community which took her in and made her one of them in difficult times.

THE FRIENDSHIP BOOK

Thursday—May 8.

EVER heard of a bus conductor turning up for work carrying a spade? I'm not sure where it happened, but it seems that the bus had a ten-minute wait at the end of its route. Usually the conductor and driver sat and chatted, or read their papers and maybe had a cup of tea from their flasks.

One day the conductor noticed a small piece of waste ground across from the bus parking place. He reckoned that with five waits a day he had nearly an hour when he could do something about it. So one sunny morning he brought his spade. Each time they arrived at the terminus he popped across and did some digging. At first his driver laughed, but one day he brought a trowel and the two men were to be seen planting pansies, lobelia and alyssum.

The little patch of waste ground became an oasis of colour—a neat and trim small garden which gave them pleasure and brightened the lives of all who passed.

Now, I was told this story by a friend who got it from another who lives in Edinburgh. Wherever it happened, I still like the idea . . .

Friday—May 9.

A FASHIONABLE London restaurant was the setting for a small family party celebrating the daughter's 21st birthday. In another corner of the same restaurant was a certain Mr Crosby.

The girl shyly took her copy of the menu over to Bing Crosby, who not only signed it but then proceeded to sing " Happy Birthday To You." Afterwards he escorted her back to her family.

It was a typical gesture from a much-loved gentleman.

THE FRIENDSHIP BOOK

Saturday—May 10.

YOU'VE had troubles? Some knocks along the way? Ponder this thought, penned by Confucius before the birth of Christ:
The gem cannot be polished without friction, nor man perfected without trials.

Sunday—May 11.

RESTORE unto me the joy of thy salvation; and uphold me with thy free spirit.

Monday—May 12.

FRITZ KREISLER was one of the world's greatest violinists.

As he grew rich and famous he played some of the finest violins ever made. Perhaps it was almost bound to happen, but it began to be said—Oh, yes, Kreisler makes wonderful music, but, of course, look at the fine instruments he plays . . .

One evening, I'm told, he was giving a concert in America, and much publicity had been given to the fact that the maestro would be playing a marvellously sweet-toned instrument by Guarnerius, one of the foremost violin-makers of all time.

At the concert that night Kreisler moved his listeners to joy and tears. As the clapping finally died away he came to the front of the platform, raised the violin above his head, then brought it down and broke it across his knee.

The audience gasped and fell silent.

Kreisler slowly looked round the hall, then smiled. " Do not worry," he said. " My Guarnerius is safe in my dressing-room. I bought this violin today in a local store for only three dollars."

Drastic measures, indeed, but he made his point.

EXPLORERS

Old houses have a lively charm
We simply can't repeat;
Who does not love to wander down
A friendly old-world street?

DAVID HOPE

THE FRIENDSHIP BOOK

Tuesday—May 13.

MANY people still remember with affection the late Tommy Handley, star of the war-time radio show "It's That Man Again." He was born in Liverpool, and always wanted to go on the stage as a professional entertainer. His 30-minute comedy show "ITMA" was listened to by some sixteen million people a week at its peak, providing laughter and light-hearted relief to many people for whom World War II and the following years brought austerity and often heartbreak.

Tommy led a hectic showbiz life, but even at the height of his career, every Thursday without fail, he sat down and wrote a letter to his mother in Liverpool—a long letter, to keep her in touch and to let her know she wasn't forgotten.

Every mother reading this will know how much these letters must have meant to her.

Wednesday—May 14.

THE deeper, richer, meaning of life is learned from its painful experiences. A man in a top hat and cloak with a lantern in his hand went through the murky streets of London to rescue destitute children. Although often reduced to his last shilling, he gave new life to thousands of little waifs. His only ambition was to help these poor children, whatever the cost to himself.

Dr Barnardo had learned the deeper meaning of trouble. When his small son died, the funeral cortège passed the funeral of a poor boy. He noticed the little coffin was without flowers, so he took some from the coffin of his own son and gave them to the bereaved mother, saying, "This is from my child to yours."

He was a great Christian gentleman.

THE FRIENDSHIP BOOK

Thursday—May 15.

A FRIEND of ours has just moved into a flat in Edinburgh. When she received letters for neighbours who've been in the building a long time, she was surprised. They, too, came knocking on her door with letters meant for her.

Then I remembered how James Lees of North Berwick told me he'd had exactly the same experience when he first went to Dundee many years ago. He had received neighbours' letters and they were getting his. Just when he thought he'd landed with a careless postman, the mistakes stopped.

Then a neighbour suggested that this was the postman's way of helping an incomer to get to know his neighbours. And many in the street had been more than a little grateful for the postman's " mistakes."

Now I know the Post Office has very strict rules about delivering letters, and I certainly don't want anyone to get into trouble, but there's a lot to be said for the friendly postman !

Friday—May 16.

JONAS CHIREMA CHIHOTA was an African chief's son who was converted by the preaching of the saintly John White of Mashonaland. After his conversion Jonas went into a neighbouring pagan village to preach the word of God. In reply they beat him and sent him home half dead.

The following Sunday he returned, preached again—and was beaten again. He offered no resistance and remained in prayer while the blows fell.

A third time he returned—and this time they did not beat him but listened to his words instead. His faith and courage had won the day.

TRUE SKILL

> *Not everyone could thatch a roof*
> *To keep it wind and waterproof;*
> *It takes the age-old craft and skill*
> *Of men who have the secret still.*

DAVID HOPE

THE FRIENDSHIP BOOK

SATURDAY—MAY 17.

YOU may find a smile in this story—and a lesson.
A neighbour's schoolgirl daughter walked up the road with me. She was looking forward to the holidays. " Sums are dead boring," she said. " For instance, Mr Gay," she went on. " If a cubic yard of earth weighs 2700 lb., what's the weight of earth in a hole one foot square by one foot deep?"

I pondered for a few moments. " One hundred pounds?" I tried.

" Wrong," she laughed. " The answer's nothing. There can't be any earth in a hole, can there?" Then she skipped off, no doubt looking for her next victim.

And the lesson?—that it pays to listen carefully, especially to a youngster!

SUNDAY—MAY 18.

IN God have I put my trust: I will not be afraid what man can do unto me.

MONDAY—MAY 19.

FOR five years Brian Barnes was a leader of the local youth club in Rossendale, Lancashire. Then he was moved to London by his employers. Before he left the area he was given a parting gift by the members of the club. What touched him most, however, was the surprise gift the young members made to his wife, and especially the note that accompanied it: " Thank you for all the time your husband has given us when he could have been with you."

Too often we admire a man for the time he gives to a good cause and forget the wife at home who supports him and makes it all possible.

THE FRIENDSHIP BOOK

TUESDAY—MAY 20.

WEDDING presents come in all shapes and sizes, and all are equally appreciated by a young couple starting out in life, but one of the most unusual ones I heard of recently occurred some time ago now. After the marriage ceremony between Sandy Murray of Achiemore in Sutherland, to Hazel Mackay of Armadale, the couple emerged from the church to the strains of the pipes.

A friend of Sandy's, old John Mackay, of Strath Halladale, was playing a special tune for them. He had composed it himself, and he had called it "Achiemore's Welcome to Hazel." It was his wedding present to Sandy and Hazel and they couldn't have had a nicer one.

WEDNESDAY—MAY 21.

I ONCE visited the church at Rye in Sussex which is often nicknamed the "Cathedral of East Sussex." Among its treasures are two very old Bibles—a "Breeches" Bible and a "Vinegar" Bible.

I thought of how the Bible, out of all the millions of books in the world, is the most beautiful. It is printed in every language, and read by scholars and little children.

The Bible is sometimes called a gilt-edged security. It has great wealth within its pages, just waiting for us to use it.

J. M. Barrie wrote about his mother, Margaret Ogilvy, and her use of the Bible : "She began the day with the New Testament in her hands . . . an old volume with its loose pages beautifully re-fixed, and its covers sewn and re-sewn by her, so that you would say it could never fall to pieces."

It never failed her. It will never fail you or me.

THE FRIENDSHIP BOOK

Thursday—May 22.

WE had some friends in the other evening, and afterwards the Lady of the House and I tidied up. I offered to do the washing-up, and started off with the glasses.

Well, you know, with all that soapy water, the glasses were a bit slippery—and the inevitable happened. One slipped out of my hand, and in trying to catch it I knocked over another.

I looked down at the pieces and wondered what the Lady of the House was going to say about that. There she was behind me, and seeing my woebegone expression, she said cheerily, " Oh, well, we'll be going metric soon, so now we have a complete set of ten !"

I brightened at once. Who else could have thought up such a consoling answer?

A toast to the ladies !

Friday—May 23.

WE forget many people we have met, but few of us, I think, ever fail to keep a picture of doctors we have known. This thought came to me the other day when I read about a retiral presentation to a doctor I once knew in a country village.

If he met you in the street he would shake your hand and say warmly, " You do look well today !"

Sometimes those of us he greeted may have been feeling a bit low, but because he said we were looking well we usually began to feel better right away !

He was a fine doctor. He used to say that humour was one of the subjects he studied when he graduated in medicine. Can you think of a better subject for a doctor, or a lawyer—or you and me—to study?

THE FRIENDSHIP BOOK

Saturday—May 24.

AND now a " musical item " from Mrs Georgina Hall. She calls it " The World of Music."

The world is full of music, the world is full of joy,
The lovely sounds of nature that nothing can destroy,
The wind that stirs the tall pine trees with sound like violins,
The chorus of awakening birds when morning light begins.
Symphonic boom of waterfall, a small stream's joyful song,
Church bells across the meadow with a call to evensong.
A childish voice in wistful prayer, a mother's tender song,
Melodies of the happy world to which we all belong.

Sunday—May 25.

CREATE in me a clean heart, O God; and renew a right spirit within me.

Monday—May 26.

SCOTSMEN are very fond of telling stories against themselves, and my friend Sandy asked me if I'd heard of the young Scots lad who wanted to impress his girl friend but just couldn't find the right words.

His English friend advised him, " I say to my wife, ' Darling, when I look into your face, time stands still.' It never fails."

Davie was very impressed and repeated the words over and over until he met his girl friend.

Before his courage left him he blurted out, " Jean, lass, when I look at your face it would stop a clock."

Sandy swears it's true, but I'm sure he had a twinkle in his eye at the time !

THE FRIENDSHIP BOOK

<u>Tuesday—May 27.</u>

AN angry customer once phoned her grocer, " I sent my son for three pounds of nuts. You gave him only two pounds. Are you sure your scales are accurate?"

The grocer promptly replied, " Madam—my scales are accurate—have you tried weighing your little boy?"

<u>Wednesday—May 28.</u>

BILL failed an important exam. He had done his best, goodness knows. He had studied as hard as anyone, swotting until all the hours. But, try as he might, he ploughed it.

He could have wept when the results reached him. It set back his career at least six months, and maybe a year. Even worse, he'd planned to get married in the autumn if all went well. Now he and his fiancée would have to think again about that, too. Yes, Bill was pretty despondent.

Then came a card from his grandmother. To his amazement, he found it was one of those which say, " Congratulations on your success ! " " Funny," he thought. " She can't have heard." But she'd heard, all right. For inside the card she had written him a note : " I know you didn't pass your exam, Bill, but you didn't fail. It's only those who don't try who truly fail." Then, underneath, were these lines :

It isn't the things you fail to do
  That should make you wipe your eye,
But the things you could and should have done,
  And simply failed to try.

With the wisdom of years, she knew that a failure is sometimes a success in disguise—and Bill, too, is beginning to understand and to hold his head high again.

THE FRIENDSHIP BOOK

Thursday—May 29.

On May 29, 1953, after a long, gruelling struggle, Edmund Hillary and Sherpa Tensing stood at last, the first men on the summit of Everest. Their oxygen was limited and they could not stay long at 29,000 feet. After he had taken the necessary photographs, Hillary saw Tensing scratch a hole in the snow and put into it a piece of chocolate and a few biscuits and sweets. They were a small gift of gratitude to the gods of Chomolungma, who, the Sherpas believed, live on the peak. Beside Tensing's offering, Hillary placed the small cross given him by John Hunt to be left on the top of Everest.

These symbols of spiritual peace and companionship, gained in the mountains by men of very different cultures, still rest, near to God, on the roof of the world.

Friday—May 30.

The Rev. Dr John Dawson Hull once said that every blade of grass was a sermon. Next day he was busy clipping his lawn when a parishioner said in passing, " That's right, Doctor, cut your sermons short!"

Saturday—May 31.

Mr ANDREW CARNEGIE was an industrialist and a multi-millionaire. General William Booth was the founder of the Salvation Army and was never a wealthy man.

Yet, oddly enough, both men attributed the secret of their success to similar ideas. Both gave the secret in a single sentence, " Hard work, taking trouble, never missing a chance."

GREAT DAYS

*While summer clouds drift idly by
Across the peaceful English sky,
Young men boast, and old men dream
Of combats on the village green.*

DAVID HOPE

JUNE

Sunday—June 1.

IF ye walk in my statutes, and keep my commandments, and do them; then I will give you rain in due season, and the land shall yield her increase.

Monday—June 2.

A LONDONER was visiting a friend in the Highlands and asked him, "Did you have much snow last winter?"

"Not very much," replied the Scot. "My neighbour had a lot more than I did."

"How could he?" queried the man from London.

"Well, he has more land than I have," explained the Scot, tongue in cheek.

Tuesday—June 3.

IT was a June evening and the Lady of the House and I were walking along a country lane. The sun was shining and a gentle breeze was blowing off a field white with clover, where cows were lying at ease.

"How contented they look," she said. "I understand just what is meant when we talk about ' living in clover.' "

How right she was ! I had never thought about the phrase, but when we got home I looked up a book about flowers—and there was the explanation, just as the Lady of the House had said.

"You must have read the book," I suggested.

She laughed and shook her head. "No," she said. "I just knew !"

Woman's intuition again !

THE FRIENDSHIP BOOK

Wednesday—June 4.

MRS ELLEN RENNISON, of 2 Bridge Bank, Walton le Dale, near Preston, must have been the proudest woman in Lancashire on the day of the school sports.

Her granddaughter, Jayne, had been looking forward to her race with all the excitement of a youngster, and when the starting whistle blew she set off at a cracking pace. Soon she was in the lead. So far in front, in fact, that she had plenty time to look over her shoulder to see how the others were doing. Then, to everyone's surprise, she began to run back down the course. As all the other girls passed her, she took the hand of the smallest girl, her friend Christine, who was last. They reached the finishing line, all smiles, and hand in hand.

Of course, Jayne didn't win a prize. But she did receive the biggest cheer of the day. And when she told Mrs Rennison that she hadn't wanted Christine to come in all on her own at the end, she also got a great big hug.

Of course, Jayne is too young to understand why her granny, with proud, happy tears in her eyes, should say, " Well done," when she'd just come in last.

But some day, maybe when she's a mother herself, I've no doubt she'll understand.

Thursday—June 5.

A POOR widow was observed to contribute a whole rouble to the funds of the Russian Bible Society.

When asked whether that sum was not rather too much for one in such poor circumstances as she was in, she answered, " Love is not afraid of giving too much."

THE FRIENDSHIP BOOK

Friday—June 6.

THE first argument after marriage can be a horror —even if it is all about nothing.

The young man stands transfixed as a steely determination appears in the previously tender eyes of his beloved. The girl watches in amazement as her gallant turns into a stubborn brute, quite unable to see her perfectly reasonable point of view.

Something like that anyway, as all who have been through it know well enough.

That's the way it was with Bill and Jane the day a friend who breeds budgies offered them one as a present. "What a beautiful blue," remarked Jane. "Green, you mean," corrected Bill from the other side of the cage. "Blue I said and blue it is." "You must be colour blind!" As both got hotter under the collar, the argument went far beyond budgies.

Then the budgie spread its wings and hopped to another perch, facing the other way. Bill and Jane were dumbfounded. The bird was two-toned, green when viewed in a certain light, and blue from a different angle.

I'm not saying Bill and Jane won't have another disagreement, but as long as they remember the two-toned budgie there's a fair chance they'll see each other's point of view.

Saturday—June 7.

THE girl of ten was explaining to her five-year-old brother why it was wrong to work on a Sunday.

"But policemen work on a Sunday," said young Albert. "Don't they go to heaven?"

The ten-year-old took it in her stride.

"Of course not," she replied. "They're not needed there!"

THE FRIENDSHIP BOOK

Sunday—June 8.

GOD is the Rock, his work is perfect: for all his ways are judgment: a God of truth and without iniquity, just and right is he.

Monday—June 9.

THE Lady of the House calls regularly on one or two not-so-very-young ladies just to see if they have any little difficulties she can sort out. Mrs Fairweather is one of her flock. The Lady of the House found her in a terrible state of worry the other day.

Her son, who works in a neighbouring town, hadn't written to her for three weeks. She knew he was going on holiday. Had something happened to him?

And Mrs Fairweather herself was trying to arrange a short holiday at the seaside. She'd known the landlady for years, but though she'd written three weeks ago she'd had no reply to her request for a booking. She was terribly afraid she'd offended the landlady in some way.

The Lady of the House volunteered to help. Two quick phone calls sorted everything out. Mrs Fairweather had got her son's holiday dates mixed. In fact, he had just returned from holiday. The very next day two delayed postcards from his holiday address dropped through her letter-box.

And the landlady was sorry she hadn't replied. But she'd had the decorators in and everything had been in a bit of a muddle. Of course, she said, she'd be delighted to see Mrs Fairweather for her holiday.

This little story doesn't prove anything. Unless perhaps to show that when we start to worry we nearly always come up with the wrong answers.

THE FRIENDSHIP BOOK

Tuesday—June 10.

MY friend Jack was telling me that he had recently moved into a new office. He likes the new premises much better than the old. " And you know what I like about them best?" he said. " We face west, so we see the most marvellous sunsets." He paused. " I'll tell you what I've realised watching these sunsets. You can't have a beautiful one without a lot of cloud. Did you ever think of that, Francis?"

I hadn't. But he's quite right, of course. Think of a glorious sunset and you think of clouds—great banks of gold. And as sunsets are enriched by clouds, so, surely, our lives are the better for some. Life without the odd cloud or two would be pretty poor and colourless, don't you think?

Wednesday—June 11.

ON JUNE 11, 1847, there died a trier — one who never knew when he was beaten. He was Sir John Franklin. As a young midshipman he had served at Copenhagen with Nelson, transcribed his famous signal at Trafalgar, then turned his attention to the long-elusive North-West Passage.

Twice he journeyed in that direction. His first trip resulted in a log of a 5000-mile journey which became a classic of its kind. His second trip added more than a thousand miles of coastline to known maps of America.

After a spell as Governor of Tasmania he set off in 1845 on his third trip in search of the North-West Passage.

It was fourteen years before it was known that he had succeeded. He did not himself survive the trip, but a search party discovered notes and cairns. The man who refused to give up had won in the end.

WILD BEAUTY

> How dull a place the world would be
> Deprived of flowers and all their graces,
> In garden, window-box or vase,
> But best of all in country places.
>
> DAVID HOPE

THE FRIENDSHIP BOOK

Thursday—June 12.

IT is sometimes difficult at first for a young wife to know how to address her newly-acquired mother-in-law. E. Nesbit, the kindly, strong-minded author of *The Railway Children* and other books, found a neat way round the problem. Her daughter-in-law had been calling her, rather formally, by her married name of " Mrs Bland." Then one day she sat down and wrote a short poem to her daughter-in-law. It read:

> " *Call me Jane or Peg or Sue,*
> *Anything but what you do!*"

So there and then it was decided—they would call each other Mil and Dil, those being the initials of " mother-in-law " and " daughter-in-law."

Rather a nice idea, don't you think?

Friday—June 13.

GENERAL MONTGOMERY was a stern disciplinarian who commanded respect wherever he went during the war.

Another side of the great man became apparent some years after, when he was in Cairo unveiling a stained-glass window dedicated to the soldiers of the Eighth Army. After a short, inspiring address he disappeared behind the altar to pull the cord. He was scheduled to reappear and lead the congregation out, but he failed to do so.

After the service the bishop went to find him. He came on the great general sitting in the vestry with tears running down his cheeks. He had broken down with grief thinking of all the fine soldiers he had known who had been killed.

As a soldier it would not have done to show emotion, but as a man he showed he cared.

THE FRIENDSHIP BOOK

Saturday—June 14.

I WAS speaking to the matron of a fine old hospital where I sometimes visit patients. Like many other people, I am always full of admiration for the cheerful, hard-working nurses. Matron told me she had been interviewing a number of girls who hoped to make nursing their career.

"What do you look for?" I asked. "How can you tell which girls will make good, dedicated nurses?"

"No problem at all," Matron laughed. "I just choose cheerful, sensible girls. They may not be dedicated when they arrive, but by the time they have worked here for a year—they will be."

Love comes with caring, doesn't it?

Sunday—June 15.

O SEND out thy light and thy truth; let them lead me.

Monday—June 16.

WHEN King Alfred the Great was in retreat at Athelney after his defeat by the Danes, a beggar came to his castle door asking for alms. His queen told King Alfred that they had only one small loaf left—not even enough for themselves and their companions.

The king replied, without hesitation, "Give the poor man half of the loaf. He who could feed the five thousand men with five loaves and two small fishes can certainly make half a loaf suffice for more than our necessities."

And so it proved. Not long afterwards, fresh provisions arrived. King Alfred's faith was proved justified.

THE FRIENDSHIP BOOK

Tuesday—June 17.

JOAN and Jane were good friends as children, and a year or so after they left school they met by chance one morning in the market place.

They started to chat about this and that, and then Joan began to bemoan the fact that she could not decide whether to buy a dress or a coat that day, not having the money for both.

Jane laughed. " I don't have that problem," she said.

" Oh," said Joan. " Do you earn such a lot of money now?"

Jane shook her head. " I haven't any at all at the moment. I haven't found a job yet, so, you see, I don't have your problem, do I?"

Joan learned a lesson that day that she was not to forget. I don't think she has grumbled since !

Wednesday—June 18.

JOHN WESLEY had a habit of getting his own way in the nicest possible manner. On one of his many journeys he had as travelling passenger in the coach a young officer whose conversation Wesley found most interesting. There was one drawback, however—the officer was inclined to swear. As they were changing vehicles for the next stage, Wesley told him how much he was enjoying his company, but added that he had a favour to ask.

" What is it?" asked the officer.

" Well," said Wesley, " as we have to travel together some distance, I beg that if I should so far forget myself as to swear, you will kindly reprove me."

Gravely the officer agreed. Never, he said afterwards, had a hint been dropped in so charming a manner.

THE FRIENDSHIP BOOK

Thursday—June 19.

TODAY, when the boundaries of right and wrong seem to have become blurred, it is sometimes difficult for young folk to know how they should run their lives.

Perhaps these thoughtful lines, written long ago by an anonymous poet, may help a little:

What is right living? Just to do your best
When worst seems easiest. To bear the ills
Of daily life with patient cheerfulness,
Nor waste dear time recounting them. To talk
Of hopeful things when doubt is in the air.
To count your blessings often, giving thanks;
To work, to love your work; to trust, to pray
For larger usefulness and clearer sight:
That is right living, pleasing in God's eyes.

Friday—June 20.

YOU'VE had a disappointment, suffered a disaster. You think all is lost. But is it? The only survivor of a shipwreck was cast ashore on a desert island. He managed to build a hut in which he kept the few possessions he had managed to save from the sinking ship. He kept praying to God for deliverance, and each day he looked out to sea hoping for a ship that would rescue him.

After an excursion in search of something to eat he came back to find that his little hut had caught fire. Everything he had saved had gone up in flames. He wept all night, bemoaning his ill-luck.

Next morning a ship lay offshore and a small boat came to take him aboard.

The captain explained, " We saw your smoke signal."

What had seemed a disaster had brought him deliverance.

THE FRIENDSHIP BOOK

Saturday—June 21.

IT'S good to see medals being pinned on to the chests of people who richly deserve them. But there are other kinds of medals, too. A Salvation Army officer once said, " My medals are on my hands," and she held out her palms, showing large, hard lumps. She explained, " I earned these cutting sandwiches and fruitcake non-stop for three days and nights, for the soldiers coming back from Dunkirk in 1940."

She was as proud of these lumps as any hero of his shiny medals.

Sunday—June 22.

GOD is our refuge and strength, a very present help in trouble.

Monday—June 23.

I OFTEN go down to the pond with some bread for the ducks. Earlier in the year I had two particular favourites in a pair of mallards, the handsome, green-headed drake and his inconspicuous little wife, who were making a nest in the reeds.

Soon the duck was ready to lay her eggs, and then, sure enough, I went down to the pond one day and there was the duck sailing across the water with a cluster of downy black chicks following behind her.

But where was Mr Drake? I ought to have known. He was hiding in the reeds waiting for his fine feathers to grow again, for the drake always loses his finery at the end of the mating season.

However, Mrs Duck was coping with her family very well on her own.

Mums usually do, don't they?

THE FRIENDSHIP BOOK

Tuesday—June 24.

DR THOMAS ALLEN, when Governor of Handsworth Methodist Theological College, once gave his students some advice. He said, "When you write an angry letter, put it under your pillow and sleep on it. In the morning, tear it up."

Wednesday—June 25.

ANGELA BURDETT-COUTTS was one of the most remarkable women this country has known. She was born an heiress. At the age of twenty-three there came to her a fortune estimated in modern terms at between thirty and forty million pounds.

She was to spend the rest of her long life using this fortune to improve the terrible conditions of slum life in Britain and helping the oppressed and the down-trodden wherever she found them. She was loved and revered by millions. "The noblest spirit we can ever know," wrote Charles Dickens. "After my mother, the most remarkable woman in the kingdom," said Edward VII.

Angela Burdett-Coutts had a deep conviction that she was directed by the hand of God to use her wealth in His service. She gave with kindness and without show and never forgot that her grandmother had been a working girl.

Today few perhaps remember her name. But when she was carried to her grave in Westminster Abbey in 1906, the crowds were six deep in the streets, and among the vast congregation were flower-girls and costermongers.

That was the recognition that would have mattered most to her—for her one desire had been to put her wealth at the service of those who needed her most.

SO SIMPLE!

*All you do is cut some stick
   And weave the bits together
And then you have a shelter strong
   Against the colder weather.
But this I have to mention still—
You need as well a deal of skill.*

DAVID HOPE

THE FRIENDSHIP BOOK

Thursday—June 26.

I WAS talking recently to a visitor from Germany. He was a schoolmaster in charge of a group of German teenagers over here on an exchange visit.

"I have seen many interesting things," he told me, "but the most moving sights of all were your War Memorials." There were tears in his eyes as he continued, "We have just the same kind of War Memorials in Germany. How tragic that our two nations should once have been enemies—and what hope there lies in the friendships now being made between our young people and yours."

What hope, indeed. Friendship is a good and glorious thing—and international friendship even greater.

Friday—June 27.

MRS FELTON is in her late seventies, and her husband, who is a few years older, is a permanent invalid, more or less confined to his chair. I met her as she was walking back home from the shops and offered to carry her basket.

Of course, in her usual independent way, she refused to let me, and began to talk about her husband.

"Oh, he's a little bit better, thank you. But I'm afraid he just sits there most of the time. You see, his mind's been affected and he lives in a world of his own." Then she added with a smile, "But, you know, the remarkable thing is that when he has his food he still says grace—and when he gives thanks his face simply lights up!"

I thought that it was, indeed, remarkable. Many a person who is fit and well has lost old Mr Felton's simple thankfulness for his daily bread.

THE FRIENDSHIP BOOK

SATURDAY—JUNE 28.

ONE of the most sacred spots in the whole of Rome is the tomb of St Paul, over which Constantine, the first Christian Emperor, built a magnificent basilica. But on the night of July 15, 1823, fire broke out in this beautiful church, destroying most of the priceless frescoes and mosaics. That same night Pope Pius VII lay on his death-bed and no one dared to tell him the distressing news of the burning church.

The loss of such a historic building was a tragic blow to Christians of all denominations. But it was decided to rebuild the great church, making it as near the original as possible. People from all over the world, in all walks of life, sent contributions. It took thirty years before the great edifice was completed. Today, St Paul's-outside-the-Wall, is one of the great attractions of Rome—a memorial not only to St Paul but also to the way we can, with His help, triumph over disaster.

SUNDAY—JUNE 29.

AND I will walk among you, and will be your God, and ye shall be my people.

MONDAY—JUNE 30.

THE little pansies in our garden are once more in bloom, and although I know that their meaning in the language of the flowers is thoughtfulness, the Lady of the House says they also mean much more.

To an older generation, she tells me, the letters of their name used to be said to stand for patience, attentiveness, neatness, sincerity, industry, earnestness and self-sacrifice.

I have a new respect for the humble pansies!

JULY

TUESDAY—JULY 1.

A FRIEND was walking along the shore of the River Tay, in Scotland.

It was a beautiful evening. The sun was warm and the sky was blue. In the bay just below the bridge that carries the railway over the river to Dundee a young man was swimming, using powerful strokes, and obviously revelling in his prowess.

Then my friend noticed a girl standing by the river, watching the swimmer. Every now and then she called out to him, guiding him in some way, even though the boy in the water seemed well able to look after himself. As he swam towards the bridge she called, "No farther that way—there are two men fishing there!"

Then my friend realised why the girl was directing him—the swimmer was blind. Jimmy Muirhead, of Newport-on-Tay, now in his twenties, has been blind since he was 17. Yet he has become one of Scotland's finest swimmers, with several gold medals to his credit.

If ever you find yourselves in deep water, not sure which way to turn, just remember Jimmy Muirhead, the boy whose courage turned tragedy into triumph.

WEDNESDAY—JULY 2.

WHEN you do a kindly deed,
 It turns into a flower seed
That grows and strengthens every day,
And spreads like blossoms on the way.
Every little thought and care
Makes happiness that others share.

THE FRIENDSHIP BOOK

Thursday—July 3.

THE Italian composer Pietro Mascagni was sitting in his study one day when a street musician stopped outside and began to play one of Mascagni's pieces on his hand-cranked barrel organ. He was turning the handle too quickly so that the tempo was faster than it should have been. Mascagni put up with it for a few minutes, then he went outside, grabbed the handle, and played the piece at its proper tempo. He then returned to his study.

Next day he was amused to see the street musician displaying a sign which read, "Pupil of the celebrated Mascagni"!

Friday—July 4.

YOUNG Mrs Benson was so miserable! Her husband had been sent on a "refresher course" by his firm and for the first time in her married life she had been left in the house on her own. The Lady of the House popped in to try to cheer her up. To her surprise, Mrs Benson met her with a smile on her face.

"I've had another visitor," she explained. "She made me feel so ashamed. But I'm so glad."

The Lady of the House couldn't quite understand what Mrs Benson meant, so she just waited.

"It was the woman from round the corner," she explained. "Her husband was killed recently in a car accident and she's left with three small daughters. To think that in her trouble she could remember to look in to see how I was! Suddenly she made me feel the luckiest woman in the world."

Mrs Benson was silent for a moment. Then she added quietly, "I think I've learned something. Perhaps the only way to cure your own unhappiness is by trying to help someone else in theirs."

THE FRIENDSHIP BOOK

Saturday—July 5.

TODAY I was riding along in the bus looking casually out of the window when a notice above a hairdresser's shop caught my eye. It simply read: No Appointment Necessary.

It set me thinking about the folk of my acquaintance who always give me a warm welcome, even when I drop in unexpectedly. Such is their hospitality that no visit, however awkwardly timed, is ever considered a nuisance. If I knock on the door, or just breeze in, they always act as though they are really pleased to see me—even if they are in the middle of their favourite television programme. Isn't that the test of true hospitality? No appointment necessary!

Sunday—July 6.

THOU wilt shew me the path of life: in thy presence is fulness of joy.

Monday—July 7.

I GET depressed by summer rain as much as anybody. How disappointing it is to see, instead of blue skies and bright sunshine, the black clouds with their promise of drizzle or downpour.

But then I think of Bob—and millions like him. Bob suffers from hay fever, an allergic reaction to grass pollen which makes his life a misery with sneezing and itching, with watery eyes and running nose. Except when there's rain about, washing away the irritating pollen and bringing him marvellous relief.

It really is true, you know, that every cloud has a silver lining.

THE FRIENDSHIP BOOK

Tuesday—July 8.

MY wife and I were once out for a country walk.

All was fine until we reached a field in the middle of which stood a huge, ferocious-looking bull. He was a full-grown bull, and he was stamping the turf within a few yards of the path.

So we decided to go round the outside of the field. It meant climbing walls and picking our way through briars and nettles, but eventually we reached the far side and were able to peer at the bull from the safety of the wall.

We now saw something we had been too nervous to notice before. The bull was firmly tethered to a stake in the ground! We could have walked safely along the path without him even being able to reach us.

Our experience provides a parable. As we go through life we often see trouble ahead. But those with the courage to press on find that things are often not as bad as they seem—once you walk right up to them!

Wednesday—July 9.

DO you know where Wordsworth saw the daffodils he wrote about in his famous poem? They were beside Ullswater, in the Lake District.

But, in fact, he saw them again and again in his memory. He would lie down to relax, he tells us, and then

> . . . *gaze upon that inward eye,*
> *Which is the bliss of solitude.*

I think that is a marvellous description of the precious gift of memory. When we are alone we can always cheer ourselves up by reliving our happiest moments. You don't have to be a famous poet to see lovely things in your mind's eye.

THE FRIENDSHIP BOOK

Thursday—July 10.

I KNOW a well-attended church whose caretaker collapsed one day from a heart attack. He eventually recovered sufficiently to resume his work, but in the intervening months the folk in the congregation did the caretaking themselves. Volunteers put their names on a list, then they took turns to do all the necessary dusting, polishing and cleaning, as well as opening and looking after the church on Sundays and for weddings, funerals and week-day meetings.

Nobody complained about the extra stint of manual work. In fact, most of them enjoyed it and took a pride in it. There is, after all, much more to church-going than just turning up for Sunday worship. As those good folk discovered, a duster or a mop and bucket are just as important as a Bible or a hymn book.

Friday—July 11.

MY desk tends to get cluttered up with a large accumulation of papers — like most desks, I suppose. Yet I am always reluctant to throw things away. Perhaps it is because I remember the story of how John Henry Newman once wrote a poetic meditation on the death of a close friend. He was not at all satisfied with the result, so he threw it away.

Fortunately for posterity, another friend happened to notice the discarded manuscript. He retrieved it and so gave to the world " The Dream of Gerontius," which was later set to music by Elgar. Millions have been uplifted by this great choral work, and especially the hymn it contains, " Praise to the Holiest in the height "—sublime words once consigned to the wastepaper basket !

THE FRIENDSHIP BOOK

Saturday—July 12.

BENJAMIN FRANKLIN was one of the liveliest personalities of 18th century America, and he had a flair for making witty remarks full of practical wisdom. He was never content just to talk, however. While men were still arguing about the nature of thunderstorms, he made his famous experiment of flying a kite amongst the thunder-clouds to prove that they were charged with electricity.

Ben Franklin was a man who liked to get things done. That is why I always think his most characteristic remark was perhaps his simplest — and his most profound:

" Well done is better than well said."

Sunday—July 13.

PRESERVE me, O God : for in thee do I put my trust.

Monday—July 14.

THE little boy had been working hard on his drawing at Sunday school, but the teacher was not at all sure that it illustrated the story she had just told. The drawing showed an aeroplane in flight, with four passengers.

" This doesn't look at all like a Bible story to me," said the teacher.

" Yes, it is !" the laddie replied. " It's the flight to Egypt."

On being asked who the figures were, he explained that they were Jesus, with Mary and Joseph, escaping from the wrath of Herod.

" But who's the fourth figure?" asked the teacher.

" Don't you know?" the little boy said, surprised. " That's Pontius—the Pilot !"

THE FRIENDSHIP BOOK

Tuesday—July 15.

I WONDER how many husbands storm off to work after sharp words at the breakfast table. I know one who doesn't—my friend Robert. He learned a tragic lesson. His father was killed on his way to work when a bus skidded on to the pavement.

To the end of her days Robert's mother regretted that though she and her husband had always lived happily together, they had parted that morning after a breakfast-table tiff.

Robert vowed that should never happen in his life. He and his wife Lilian have a pact that they will never end the day or part from each other if a quarrel has not been made up.

"And you know," said Robert, "probably because we have that pact it's very seldom we have a quarrel. Do you believe that, Francis?"

I do.

Wednesday—July 16.

PICTURE a shabby bedroom in a Manchester boarding-house in 1847. A minister is staying there, recovering from an operation which has just been performed to remove a cataract. There is every chance that he will never be able to see again.

Looking after him is his eldest daughter, herself suffering from raging toothache. The postman arrives with a parcel. It is her first novel—rejected by yet another publisher. What a depressing scene!

But the daughter immediately sits down to write another and better novel. It is as though she wants to show the world how to triumph over misfortune. Her name was Charlotte Bronte, and the novel she began on such a dismal day was that great story, "Jane Eyre."

THE FRIENDSHIP BOOK

Thursday—July 17.

I LIKE a story with a twist in the tail. Like the events in the last film made by the veteran French actor, Jean Gabin. He played the part of a criminal who escaped from prison and eventually arrived in Rome to recover the stolen gold he had buried under a lemon tree.

Disguised as a bishop, he reached the hiding-place, only to find that the tree had disappeared and that nearby stood a beautiful modern church. He went inside and asked the priest if he remembered the lemon tree.

" Very well indeed," said the priest. " It was struck by lightning—an act of God, you might say. When we dug it up we found gold buried beneath its roots, and with it we built this fine new church."

On his way out the mock bishop, now resigned to his loss, was asked if he would like to put anything into the offertory.

" No," he said. " I've given enough already !"

Friday—July 18.

THERE are various ways of keeping would-be interrupters quiet. I love the story Mr Edward Heath tells about a meeting he had with the Governor of one of the African colonies once administered by Britain.

" Sir William Twining, one of the old school, with a lively sense of humour, planted us in the chairs around him in the study, then offered us large lumps of toffee.

" ' I find it prevents interruptions to my speech,' he explained."

Then he laid down the law about how the colony should be run, without interference from his visitors !

THE FRIENDSHIP BOOK

Saturday—July 19.

CAN you recognise opportunity when it presents itself to you?

A Greek sculptor once did a statue which he called Opportunity.

It stands on tiptoe to show how short a time it lingers; it has wings on its feet for it can fly quickly away; its front hair is long in order that men can seize it as it passes; the back of its head is bald because once past it can never be caught.

Sunday—July 20.

JUDGE not, and ye shall not be judged: condemn not, and ye shall not be condemned.

Monday—July 21.

ABOUT a hundred years ago an evangelist was singing a hymn on a steamer sailing down the River Potomac in the United States. A man pushed through the crowd and asked the singer if he had fought in the Civil War some fifteen years previously. When the two men compared notes it was found that the evangelist had one night been on sentry duty. The other man was an enemy sniper, ready to shoot him down. His rifle was aimed and he was about to fire when the sentry started singing a well-known hymn. He reached the words:

"*Cover my defenceless head*
With the shadow of Thy wing."

Immediately the sniper lowered his rifle, quite unable to shoot.

This famous hymn must have brought peace and comfort to millions more. Do you recognise these lines? They are, of course, from Charles Wesley's " Jesu, Lover of my soul."

PLEASURES

*Summer days are all too short
For lively children fond of sport:
Sights to see and things to do,
Lots of fun for parents, too!*

*When bleak winter looms again
We endure the fog and rain,
Dreaming, though our hands are numb,
Of golden summers still to come.*

DAVID HOPE

THE FRIENDSHIP BOOK

Tuesday—July 22.

WE were all sitting down to tea when Jimmy leaned over and took the largest piece of cream cake from the far side of the table.

"That's not very polite," said his little sister. "I never take the biggest piece. I always take the smallest."

"That's all right then," said Jimmy. "'Cos I've left it for you!"

Wednesday—July 23.

THE former Speaker of the House of Commons, Lord Selwyn Lloyd, was a Foreign Secretary at a controversial period in British politics. He had many critics, and even some of his own colleagues had little good to say about his actions.

Many years later, when asked if he had any hard feelings about those who had attacked him, he shook his head and replied, "Forgiveness is the most effective form of revenge."

And the only form worth taking.

Thursday—July 24.

THE golfer was having a terrible round, splaying balls everywhere but down the fairway.

At the last hole he again drove hard, but wide. His ball hurtled towards the road and smashed a passing car's windscreen. The startled driver put on his brakes, realised what had happened, and marched determinedly up to the golfer.

"What are you going to do about it?" he asked angrily.

Sadly the golfer looked down at the club he was still holding. "I think," he said, "I'll have to change my grip."

THE FRIENDSHIP BOOK

Friday—July 25.

ONE day in 1571 Captain William Slingsby was riding across a rough Yorkshire common when his horse stumbled. Dismounting to discover the reason why, Slingsby noticed a small spring of water. When he drank from it he was surprised to find that it tasted like the water of fashionable springs on the Continent, especially those at Spa in Belgium.

So he had the area paved and walled, and began to publicise this as "the English Spa," encouraging ordinary people to drink the health-giving waters. Eventually, from this small beginning, there developed the town of Harrogate, for centuries famous as a health resort and whose Royal Bath Hospital still specialises in the treatment of rheumatic diseases. Thus one practical, public-spirited man helped bring healing to multitudes of people.

Saturday—July 26.

ARE you holidaying abroad this year?
Then you may like to hear the story about the old lady at the airport who went aboard the plane and told the flight steward that it was her very first trip. It wasn't an ideal night for a first flight. There was thunder about and the rain was lashing down on the plane as it taxied to the end of the runway.

Breaking a strict rule, the steward unfastened his seat belt and sat on the arm of her seat, taking her hand in his. She squeezed his hand tight and held on. Once the plane was safely aloft and the steward started back to his own seat, she turned to him and whispered:

"Now, son, if you're afraid when we go to land, you come right back here and I'll hold your hand again!"

THE FRIENDSHIP BOOK

Sunday—July 27.

BLESSED are ye that hunger now: for ye shall be filled. Blessed are ye that weep now: for ye shall laugh.

Monday—July 28.

JENNIE LIND was a singer of world-wide fame in the early part of this century when suddenly she retired from the stage and nobody knew the reason. A friend, visiting her one day, found her seated in her beautiful garden in the country and asked her why she had retired at the height of a successful career.

The great singer smiled and confessed, pointing to the quiet scene around, " It was because my busy, whirlwind life was making me forget God and all this."

Realising what she was missing, she had turned her back on the glitter and excitement and found what her life was lacking—contentment.

Tuesday—July 29.

THE writer, Sir James Barrie, was at a family picnic. After tucking in heartily, one of the little boys was making quick work of a box of chocolates. His mother told him that he would be sick the next day if he ate any more chocolates. The youngster promptly took another, saying, " I shall be sick tonight."

Barrie was so amused by the line that he afterwards resolved to use it in *Peter Pan* and he offered the boy a royalty of one halfpenny a performance for the copyright. The little boy accepted at once. Such an investment must have proved worth an upset tummy!

THE FRIENDSHIP BOOK

Wednesday—July 30.

IT is often among the very old that we find the courage that is born of faith. A friend has been telling me of one old lady in the Second World War who never went to the shelter during an air raid. Asked why, she replied, " I just say my prayers and go to sleep. There is no need for *both* of us to stay awake."

Thursday—July 31.

REDUNDANCY is a newish word, but the problem has been with us for some time.

Many years ago a Scottish handweaver told his ten-year-old son, " We'll have to go to America. This new machinery has put me out of a job. I know only the old ways of weaving."

So the family moved from Dunfermline to a small town near Pittsburgh, where the boy and his father got jobs in a cotton mill. Six years later the father died, and to support his mother and younger brother the boy became a telegraph message boy, studying every night to learn more about the railways.

He was made assistant superintendent, and, aware of how the railway was expanding, invested his savings in a venture for making sleeping cars. He invested the profit in oil lands, then turned his attention to the steel industry.

Well, in the end he built a massive fortune, and, giving away more than 350 million dollars to help others, became the world's best-known philanthropist.

Odd, isn't it, that Andrew Carnegie put to work the same sort of machinery that forced his father out of a job—and used its fruits for the benefit of mankind.

AUGUST

Friday—August 1.

WHICH of the instruments of the orchestra is most difficult to play?

If you ask any knowledgeable musical friends you're sure to start an argument, with some plumping for the harp, others voting for the oboe or French horn. But the late Sir Malcolm Sargent had quite a different answer. In his dressing-room before the last night of the Proms one year he was asked that same question. Fingering the elegant carnation in his buttonhole, he pondered.

"Without doubt, it is the second violin. I can find any number of violinists who can perform the job of being lead or first violin admirably." And his bright eyes twinkled. "But it takes a rare type of ability to play the second fiddle with enthusiasm."

Sir Malcolm's words held a deeper meaning, of course.

The world couldn't exist without its second fiddles. Think of the people who never hit the headlines but cheerfully suppress their own ambitions to help a husband or support a family. While the stars receive the flowers and the plaudits, the second fiddles soldier on in the background, doing a good job and often getting very little thanks for it.

Spare a thought for them. Sir Malcolm did!

Saturday—August 2.

WHAT is wealth? It's not such a simple question as it sounds. "The measure of a man's wealth," said a wise man, "is not the plenitude of his possessions but the fewness of his wants."

THE FRIENDSHIP BOOK

Sunday—August 3.

AND as ye would that men should do to you, do ye also to them likewise.

Monday—August 4.

MY thanks to the Rev. John Taylor for this definition of a grandmother as seen through the eyes of any eight-year-old :

A grandmother is a lady who has no children of her own, so she likes other people's little girls and boys. A grandfather is a man grandmother. He goes for walks with the boys and talks about fishing and tractors. But grandmothers don't have to do anything — just be there.

Usually they are fat, but not too fat to tie children's shoes. They wear glasses and funny underwear, and they can take their teeth out. They don't have to be clever, only answer questions like, "Why do dogs hate cats?" They don't baby-talk like visitors. When they read to us they don't miss bits out or mind if it's the same story over again. Everybody should have a grandmother, especially if you don't have television.

Tuesday—August 5.

AN exasperated salesman abandoned his car in a "No Parking" area and left a note, "I've circled this block twenty times. I have an appointment and must keep it or lose my job. Forgive us our trespasses."

He returned to find a ticket under his wiper blade with another note appended by the traffic warden : "I've circled this block twenty years. If I don't give you a ticket I'll lose my job. Lead us not into temptation."

THE FRIENDSHIP BOOK

Wednesday—August 6.

I WAS feeling rather down in the dumps when I was introduced to Jim. For one thing, I had a headache, and I had all sorts of problems on my mind. Jim, on the other hand, didn't seem to have a care in the world. He was a man of about sixty, grey-haired, red-cheeked and all smiles, happily doing some gardening to help the friend at whose house we called.

I left feeling rather envious. Lucky Jim! How nice it must be to have no worries! Then I noticed in a car outside the house a young man who was so severely handicapped that he could do little more than sit there. I was told that this was Jim's son, a spastic who required constant attention.

It occurred to me that Jim had far greater problems than I had, yet he managed to keep cheerful and give the impression that all was well. Now, every time I think about him, I feel that little bit brighter myself!

Thursday—August 7.

IN an odd corner of a parish magazine I noticed the following little paragraph about how the Bible tells us God called the following people to his service:

Moses, when he was busy with his flock;
Gideon, when he was busy threshing wheat;
Elisha, when he was busy ploughing;
Peter and Andrew, when they were busy fishing;
James and John, when they were busy mending their nets;
Matthew, when he was busy collecting taxes.

Do you see the point it illustrates? When you want to get something done it is usually best to ask somebody who is already busy.

FREEDOM

The scents from a well-stocked garden,
The sound of the restless sea,
Lie deep in our memories' storehouse
Wherever we chance to be,
Calling up happy visions
Of days that are glad and free.

DAVID HOPE

THE FRIENDSHIP BOOK

Friday—August 8.

DAME FLORA ROBSON was once asked how her religion had helped her in her long stage career. She answered:

"I have learned that we should ask God's blessing on our work—but never ask Him to do it for us. When I approach a new part I go all out to master it, so that I can feel that whatever happens I have no reason to blame myself. Then, just before the first performance I say a little prayer: 'I've done all I can, Father—please take over now and give me inspiration.' This makes all the difference."

Saturday—August 9.

I WAS looking round a fascinating museum in Whitby, the little town on the Yorkshire coast famous for its association with Captain Cook. I noticed in a glass case an 18th century manual of navigation—the book from which the great explorer learnt how to handle a ship and charter unknown oceans.

What struck me was that the book was open at a section entitled, "Plain Sailing." It had never occurred to me before that this was a technical term for an art which has to be learnt.

So I left the museum reflecting that life is never as easy as we would like to think. Even when the stormy waters seem to be all behind us we still have to behave with commonsense and tact, never underestimating the difficulty of just "plain sailing."

Sunday—August 10.

THEY that are whole need not a physician; but they that are sick.

THE FRIENDSHIP BOOK

Monday—August 11.

THE greatest of men are nearly always the most humble.

Isaac Newton is remembered chiefly for observing a falling apple and thus discovering the law of gravity. He also did many other things—he became a Member of Parliament, Master of the Mint, and taught us how the rainbow gets its colours.

But when a friend complimented him on all the new light which he had thrown upon science, Sir Isaac replied quietly, " I am only like a child picking up pebbles on the shore of the great ocean of truth."

Tuesday—August 12.

OTTO KLEMPERER, who died in 1972 at the age of 87, was not just a very great conductor; he was a man with the most tremendous determination to triumph over misfortune. In 1931 the Nazis confiscated his property and would have thrown him into a concentration camp if he had not managed to escape to the United States. In 1938 he had an operation to remove a brain tumour, which left him partially paralysed, so that he could no longer hold the conductor's baton in his right hand. Undaunted, he conducted with his left, and went on to give brilliant concerts throughout the world.

In 1951 he fell and badly fractured his hip. From now on he would never be able to stand for any length of time. So he arranged to conduct his orchestras sitting down. I shall not forget the sight of that gaunt old man in front of the London Philharmonic Orchestra, conducting from a chair —with his left hand! Otto Klemperer will always be remembered as much for his courage as for his music.

THE FRIENDSHIP BOOK

Wednesday—August 13.

SOME folk have an almost superstitious attitude towards the Bible, opening it at random and thrusting in a finger in the hope that they will find a helpful text. If you are tempted to try this, instead of disciplined Bible-reading, always remember the following story :

A man in need of advice opened his Bible and put his finger by chance on the text, " And Judas went and hanged himself." He shut the Bible and tried again. This time he hit upon the words, " Go and do thou likewise." Hoping for something better, he tried a third time, and found, " What thou doest, do quickly."

Thursday—August 14.

WE had gone to visit Dorothy, who had recently lost her husband after a long and painful illness. As we were leaving we noticed on the sideboard a particularly fine photograph of Dorothy and her late husband.

" That's a good photo of Ron, isn't it?" she said rather proudly. " You won't have seen this one before—I'll tell you why."

Dorothy explained that this was a special portrait they had once had taken—just a close-up of the two of them together. They had made a vow that they would put it on display only when either one of them died. Then it would remind whichever partner was left of their happy married life, and also comfort them with the Christian hope of reunion in the life beyond.

We thought it was a splendid idea. Dorothy was facing up to the hurt of separation, feeling sure that it was only temporary. In that photograph she was still happily married to her beloved Ron.

RURAL RETREAT

> *Thank God for old-time villages*
> *On pleasant summer days,*
> *With restful hospitality*
> *And simple country ways.*

DAVID HOPE

THE FRIENDSHIP BOOK

Friday—August 15.

PEGGY and Bill were only ten and eight years old when their parents died.

Their grandmother was a pensioner, but there was no question in her mind that it was her responsibility to bring up the bewildered orphans.

To make ends meet, Granny Smith had to go out cleaning at odd hours. But Peggy and her young brother always felt aware of her presence through the notes she left them all over the house.

Propped up on the kitchen table would be, " Peggy—casserole's all ready in oven. Just switch on to 350° at 4.30." On an inside page of Bill's comic might be pinned, " Now, now, William—you can read this *after* you've done your homework ! "

Even when Gran had gone, she lived on in the house. In the oddest places would be found hidden away little notes of encouragement and advice, in dictionaries, cook books, drawers.

When Peggy got engaged she shed a quiet tear at the thought that neither her mother nor Gran would ever know the man she loved. Later, she was searching in the attic for Gran's wedding veil which Peggy's mother had worn as well. She planned to wear it as her " something old."

She drew out the veil and there was a note which read simply, " Lots of luck, Peggy. I'm sure I'd love him, too."

A loving heart is a joy for ever !

Saturday—August 16.

IN trying hard for peace of mind,
  Some hint of sunshine you will find.
You say you can't believe this true?
Think of others, what they've lived through !

THE FRIENDSHIP BOOK

Sunday—August 17.

AND when they had brought their ships to land, they forsook all, and followed him.

Monday—August 18.

IN his book *The Long Journey*, Sidney Poitier, the coloured actor, relates how at the age of 18 he arrived in New York with hardly any money. He thought that he would be able to rent a cheap room, but the landlords wanted more than he had, so he spent many nights sheltering in a bus terminal. When the weather grew warmer he slept in the open, covering himself with newspaper.

Money was not his only problem; he was terribly lonely. He had had only one full year's schooling and could not read. His strong West Indian accent seemed to act as a barrier. Years later, when he received an Oscar for a great acting performance, he smiled as he said, " It has been a long journey to this moment."

His perseverance and dedication had overcome all obstacles.

Tuesday—August 19.

TOM HARVEY, who lives in the Kingsbury district of North-west London, wrote to tell me about the Whistling Postman. His name is Len Findlay, and he has a delivery round there. Mr Harvey says that not only does Len whistle while he works, but he sometimes serenades, too. If he notices someone receiving a batch of birthday cards, Len can't resist breaking into voice with, " Happy Birthday To You !"

It's a service the British Post Office might well be proud of !

AGE AND BEAUTY

*Great castles in their grim old age
May dwell with beauty, too,
And we who glance at history's page
Can still enjoy the view,*

As men have done through ages past
  With patriotic pride,
For Nature's scenic glories last
  Though countless men have died.

DAVID HOPE

THE FRIENDSHIP BOOK

Wednesday—August 20.

WHAT would you do if you learned you were to die at sunset? That was the question St Francis of Assisi was asked one afternoon as he was tending his garden.

"I would finish hoeing my garden," he replied simply.

To me, this seems the supreme answer to all the troubled young folk who are setting off in life in a world that appears to hold little security for them. We can't be sure of anything, they say, not now or next year or the year after. So why should we bother trying to make a life for ourselves? Why bother to study for exams or get married or have children?

St Francis put his answer in a simple metaphor. Go on hoeing your garden. The task is still there—the seed to plant, the home to build, the book to write, the exam to prepare for. If the morning looks dark, well, so did the morning before the first Christmas.

Whatever life holds in store, we'll meet it all the better if we have fulfilled the present to the best of our ability. Today is still ours—along with the responsibility of living it to the full.

Thursday—August 21.

THE Lady of the House had dropped into a coffee shop the other morning. When she came home she was still smiling over a bit of conversation overheard from the next table. A woman had joined her friend who was sitting waiting for her.

"Sorry I'm later than usual, love," she said, "but my dishwasher wouldn't work this morning."

"Oh, dear," said the other. "What's wrong with him?"

THE FRIENDSHIP BOOK

Friday—August 22.

BENJAMIN FRANKLIN once demonstrated the result of an over-abundance of plenty. A small boy and his mother were visiting the famous man and Dr Franklin took an apple from a dish and gave it to the child. The little boy beamed with delight although he could hardly hold the apple in his little hands. Then Dr Franklin gave the child another apple—and the child smiled even more.

Then Dr Franklin took a bigger, brighter apple from the bowl and held it out for the youngster. Try as he might, the little boy could not hold three apples and he dropped them all and burst into tears.

Two apples would have been happiness enough.

Saturday—August 23.

I HAVE been hearing about a little-known heroine, Ruth Stranex, who, a few years ago, was a missionary in Uganda, working as a sister in the Christian hospital at Amudat. In the midst of her work she was suddenly arrested, taken 350 miles to prison, and locked in a small, insanitary cell.

Prayer and Bible-reading provided strength for the ordeal, but above all she was uplifted by a colleague and friend called Anne, who followed her to the prison and did everything possible to help. In her prison cell Ruth went down on her knees and thanked God for friends.

A few days later she was released, only to be deported shortly afterwards and forced to leave the African people she had grown to love. But Ruth has always treasured the memory of Anne's support throughout her frightening experience.

She learned then, as so many have before, the extraordinary power of friendship and the strength that can flow from one person to another.

THE FRIENDSHIP BOOK

Sunday—August 24.

MAN shall not live by bread alone, but by every word of God.

Monday—August 25.

PEOPLE who lead busy lives are apt to consider the telephone a curse rather than the blessing it was meant to be. After all, there is nothing more exasperating than to be sitting down to a meal, or to be having a nap by the fireside—and the phone rings.

But some folk are delighted every time they hear it. They are the lonely, house-bound people—like Mrs Benson, for example. She is 85, and quite crippled with arthritis. I happened to learn that it was her birthday today, so I gave her a ring. Just a few words of greeting, and a brief conversation—yet it seemed to mean so much to her.

It's true, you know, you really can cheer somebody up by making a phone call. Try it!

Tuesday—August 26.

IT is a good thing for us to count our blessings and to be genuinely grateful for the simple things which we so often take for granted. Such a man was the great English poet John Milton. In a little poem, which we now use as a hymn, he wrote:
Let us with a gladsome mind
Praise the Lord for He is kind . . .
All things living He doth feed,
His full hand supplies their need.

Milton wrote those lines in 1645. Seven years later he was totally blind. But he clearly remembered all the beauty he had enjoyed—and he never lost his sense of gratitude for the good things of life.

FRIENDS

Making a bright day even brighter,
Making a glad heart even lighter,
Chasing all cares and worries away —
Friends can do that any day!

DAVID HOPE

THE FRIENDSHIP BOOK

Wednesday—August 27.

MRS SMITHSON is a sprightly old lady of 87 who lives with just a little dog to keep her company. When we heard that she had fallen down the stairs and broken her leg, we really felt it was unlikely she would ever return from hospital. But such is her spirit that she got back home, and with the district nurse, meals-on-wheels and a helping hand from neighbours, she was soon on her feet again.

I met her today, limping down the street to post a letter.

" It's a great day !" she exclaimed. " Aren't you going to congratulate me?"

I hesitated, wondering what she meant.

" Can't you see ? It's my first time without a stick !"

And off she hobbled, as happy as any toddler just learning to walk!

Thursday—August 28.

TODAY I saw an exceptionally fine piece of carving — that of a warship in the old sailing days, complete with masts, rigging, cabins, port holes and so forth, with every tiny detail faithfully reproduced. At first I thought it was made of ivory. Then I was told that it had been carved from bones. Not bone—but odd bones, left over from small rations of meat or poultry.

You see, this intricate and graceful model had been made over many weary months by French prisoners captured during the Napoleonic Wars. An inspiring example, showing how even odd scraps may be turned — in the midst of a life of monotony and restriction — into something of lasting beauty.

THE FRIENDSHIP BOOK

Friday—August 29.

SOME joy, some love, some quiet content,
  Some peace, some understanding,
Some help, some kindness, I can give,
  And give without demanding,
To folk about me, troubled souls,
  The lonely and the grieving,
My heart is blessed in giving thus—
  May theirs be in receiving.

Saturday—August 30.

It is not often that a man writes his own epitaph, but here is one written by a former captain of a slave ship who died in 1807 :

" *Once an infidel and libertine,*
A servant of slaves in Africa:
Was by the rich mercy of our Lord and Saviour
Preserved, restored, pardoned,
And appointed to preach the Faith
He had long laboured to destroy."

His name was John Newton, vicar of St Mary Woolnoth, London—better known as the author of several well-loved hymns, such as " How sweet the name of Jesus sounds " and " Glorious things of thee are spoken." When these are sung by the average congregation, how many, I wonder, realise that they were penned by " the old African blasphemer," as he once called himself.

John Newton is the classic example of a changed man, a shining example of how it is always possible to make a fresh start.

Sunday—August 31.

My soul doth magnify the Lord, and my spirit hath rejoiced in God my Saviour.

LEARNING

*The hardy men who heave their nets
And bring their catch to port
Began their fishing, don't forget,
As boys who fished for sport.*

DAVID HOPE

SEPTEMBER

Monday—September 1.

I HEARD recently of a convict who wore, under his uniform, a suit of shining armour. A weekly newspaper had published a letter appealing for toys for needy children. Many people must have read the letter, but only one replied — the convict who was serving a long term of imprisonment in Parkhurst Prison on the Isle of Wight.

He saved up his pocket money, bought materials to make toys and sent them for the children. When he was offered something to help cover the cost of the materials he would accept nothing.

Do you wonder that, despite the uniform he wore, I say he was a knight in shining armour?

Tuesday—September 2.

I CONFESS that I have never found writing particularly easy. To produce something that is worth while and readable, any writer has to work hard on his research and the sheer craftsmanship of shaping the sentences. So when I find that writing is becoming difficult I think of men like Bill Sayers, who is paralysed from the shoulders down as a result of polio.

Bill has published an account of his many years in an iron lung, and still toils away at his writing. He manages it by using a mouth-stick, with which he works an electric typewriter. To type a complete page takes him twenty minutes.

The thought of such patience and courage makes all my problems as a writer seem trivial. Handicapped folk like Bill have so much to teach those of us who are fit and well.

THE FRIENDSHIP BOOK

Wednesday—September 3.

IN the floor at the west entrance of St Ethelburga's Church in Bishopsgate, London, there is a Latin inscription which reads, " Come in good—go out better." And it always reminds me of Emma's store. It's in a Northumberland village, and I remember very clearly my first visit to it. It was dark inside, and the floor was covered with sacks of flour, hen corn and dog biscuits. As my eyes adjusted to the gloom a voice from a back room said, " I can't walk far—come through, dear. Would you like a cup of tea? Help yourself to ginger cake."

It was old Emma herself. I sat down and thought that I was about to hear all her troubles—but I was wrong. I found that Emma served the villagers not only with groceries but by listening to *their* troubles. Her home was a place of affection and security, where others found a warm and friendly welcome.

There was no Latin inscription on Emma's floor, only sacks—but I went in good and I came out better.

Thursday—September 4.

WHAT I like best about children is their directness. And have you noticed how the very young and the very old understand one another so perfectly?

One old granny I know was not the least bit put out when young Jenny suddenly asked her, " Are you very old?"

Granny simply put down her knitting for a moment, smiled into Jenny's eyes, and said, " No, dear, I wouldn't say I was old, exactly. But I must admit I've been young for a long, long time !"

THE FRIENDSHIP BOOK

Friday—September 5.

SOME folk think autumn rather a sad time because it heralds the approach of winter. The thought crossed my mind as I sat in the garden one day, enjoying the September sunshine. Then I noticed a peacock, one of my very favourite creatures. Not the well-known bird, but the peacock butterfly — a magnificent specimen which was visiting our last display of flowers in the border.

To my great joy it came and settled on my sleeve and I was able to admire at close quarters the splendour of its wings . . . the two brilliant "eyes," like those on a peacock's tail, brilliant splashes of blue and bronze, the delicate markings of harmonious colours.

After a few seconds it flew away. But it left me with a feeling of hope. Winter will come, I know. And yet, after the winter, the flowers and butterflies will be back again to fill the world with beauty.

Saturday—September 6.

MR SMITH suddenly announced at breakfast that he didn't have to go to the office that morning.

"Listen," said his wife, "don't think you're going to run off and play golf and leave me with all this work."

"Golf is the furthest thing from my mind," protested her husband. "Now, will you please pass the putter?"

Sunday—September 7.

GIVE ear, O ye heavens, and I will speak; and hear, O earth, the words of my mouth.

THE FRIENDSHIP BOOK

Monday—September 8.

A LITTLE boy once lived in a one-roomed house with his father who was a shoemaker. He didn't like going to school ; he much preferred to play with a toy theatre he had made or to write fairy tales.

He even tried to sing his tales, but, bless you, he couldn't sing. He couldn't dance either. In fact, there didn't seem to be very much that he *was* capable of doing. But he was always interested in fairy tales, and wrote tale after tale after tale—until they were being asked for all over Europe.

So throughout his life Hans Christian Andersen continued writing those fairy tales which have entranced girls and boys ever since.

Tuesday—September 9.

I HAVE just been re-reading *Doctor Sangster*, the biography of the great Methodist evangelist, so movingly written by his son Paul. In stark contrast to his amazingly active life as an energetic minister, tirelessly travelling and preaching, the final months were of absolute weakness and immobility caused by the mystery disease of muscular atrophy.

Dr Sangster faced this devastating illness with inspiring courage. In a final attempt to find a cure he had gone with his wife to the Neurological Clinic at Freudenstadt in the Black Forest. But nothing could be done for him. "The superintendent wept," writes Paul, " as he told my mother he could not help." Then he adds, of his courageous father, " The patient comforted him."

Let us be thankful that so often we find patients like Dr Sangster, who sometimes show more faith and fortitude than those who minister to them.

THE FRIENDSHIP BOOK

Wednesday—September 10.

JUST over a hundred years ago Robert Louis Stevenson visited Edinburgh Royal Infirmary to see a doctor friend.

He passed a burly young man limping along on crutches, his one leg swathed in bandages. As Robert watched, the man sought out every child in bed, and had them chuckling at his imitation of a pirate. Robert was then introduced to the one-legged man, William Ernest Hanley from London. Like R.L.S., he was a writer. Like him, he'd a history of illness.

As a boy, William had had a foot amputated because of tuberculosis in the bones. In his twenties, while struggling to make a living, he was told the other foot would also have to be amputated.

William used all his savings to travel to Edinburgh to consult Sir Joseph Lister. Lister saved his foot, but the operation was painful. Jobless, moneyless, crippled and in great pain, William spent his convalescence doing his best to cheer up sick children. He knew only too well how they felt.

He also inspired Robert Louis Stevenson. He put William into a book, not as the hero, but as a pirate—a pirate with one leg, a winning personality, a sense of humour and an unconquerable spirit. And he called him Long John Silver. Thus was born the most lovable villain in all literature.

Thursday—September 11.

JACK and Jenny were playing happily with their toy telephones with their mummy. Suddenly she noticed what time it was, dialled them both and told them it was bath-time.

"Sorry," said Jack firmly, replacing the receiver, "wrong number!"

THE FRIENDSHIP BOOK

Friday—September 12.

THE late Pope Paul, who died in 1978, left behind many memories of his compassion and love.

Once, after giving the blessing in St Peter's Square, he was being carried out when he noticed a group of handicapped children. He motioned that he wanted to go down to talk with them, which he did. Unhappily, one youngster in a wheelchair wasn't able to come nearer. So this eighty-year-old man, badly crippled by arthritis, got off his throne and knelt down beside the little boy in the wheelchair.

Saturday—September 13.

SOMETIMES we know we should apologise for something said or done—yet how difficult it can be. In the years just after the last war, Don Whyte, a well-known Scottish journalist, became very friendly with a young German who had been captured by the Allies when he was only sixteen.

One night Don took the young German home. His father, who harboured hard thoughts about the Germans, was furious and showed it, and the young German, who had taken so little part in the war, was deeply hurt.

When he thought about it, Don's father realised that he was being unreasonable. He wanted to apologise, but could not put it into words.

In silence he went to the piano and began to play one of the most beautiful works of Schubert. As the German listened, his eyes met those of the player. An unspoken message passed between the two. Without a word having been uttered, an apology was given and accepted.

Of course, we can't all set our apologies to music, but there is always a way—if we really want to find one.

THE FRIENDSHIP BOOK

Sunday—September 14.

THE Lord he is God in heaven above, and upon the earth beneath : there is none else.

Monday—September 15.

"WHAT do you make of this?" asked the Lady of the House.

She wrote the following on a memo pad— *Faults Husband Quarrel Wife Faults.*

Well, what do you make of it? After studying it for a minute or two I had to confess myself baffled. So she explained it to me.

"It simply means," she said, "that in a quarrel between husband and wife, *there are faults on both sides.*"

Easy once you see it—and worth thinking about, too!

Tuesday—September 16.

MYRA is headmistress of a large comprehensive school and leads a very busy life. She does not have much time to devote to her various hobbies, but when she goes on holiday her tapestry work goes, too. It does not progress very quickly, but when she does have a little spare time, well, it is always there, like an old friend. A little flower was completed one Christmas when she stayed with an aunt, and a heraldic beast reminds her of a visit to Cornwall.

She told me once that she sees her tapestry as rather like life itself—there is the background, which is rather dull, and the coloured bits that are fun. Not until she gets to the end and the whole pattern is complete will the picture be seen properly.

So, until then, every single stitch counts.

THE FRIENDSHIP BOOK

Wednesday—September 17.

PAULA YOUNG was married to a soldier stationed in Germany. She's in her twenties, so her only knowledge of the last war came from stories she's heard or books she's read. Then the Youngs decided to visit Arnhem and see the famous bridge.

As they approached Arnhem they saw a sign giving directions to a war cemetery, and they decided to have a look. In a shady grove near the road Paula could see row upon row of sparkling white headstones. There were fresh flowers at each of the 200 graves.

" We walked slowly round," wrote Paula, " with singing birds the only sound to be heard, and I read out the inscriptions to my two children. What really surprised me was the ages of the men who'd fallen—eighteen and nineteen—just at the beginning of life.

" In the beautiful little shelter was a visitors' book. With tears in my eyes I read some of the remarks of people from all over the world. But most were from the Dutch, who'd written in their own language, ' Thank you for our freedom.'

" I was proud to add our names to the list. I found it hard to express exactly what I felt, but here is what I wrote : ' May our generation never forget that they gave their all for us.' "

A prayer we all echo silently on this 36th anniversary of the Battle of Arnhem.

Thursday—September 18.

AN elderly woman in a Bournemouth hotel was heard to remark to a friend, " I never tell anyone how old I am, dear. When you get to my age, actions creak louder than words!"

THE FRIENDSHIP BOOK

Friday—September 19.

DO you remember that part in *The Count of Monte Cristo*, by Alexander Dumas, where the Count is tunnelling through solid rock in an attempt to escape from the notorious prison of the Chateau d'If? Utterly exhausted, and feeling his task is hopeless, he cries out:

" O God, let me not die here in despair !"

Then he hears a voice from quite close by—the voice of the old priest with whom he eventually changes places and so manages to escape:

" Who is this, who speaks of God and despair in the same breath?"

He was right, of course. With God all things are possible. While there's faith, there's hope.

Saturday—September 20.

ALFRED BIRD was a chemist. To those who came to his shop in Birmingham it must have seemed he hadn't a care in the world. He had a good business, a fine reputation, and money in the bank. But Alfred had one cloud in his sky—his wife was delicate. Certain things she ate made her very ill, and the doctors could do little to help her.

So Alfred decided to invent something which she could eat, something that she would enjoy. I don't know how long it took him, but I can picture the day when he brought through a plate, set it before her, and watched with pride while she took her first taste.

On that day in 1837 I'm sure neither of them could have known Alfred's invention would be famous, or that it would go on to make a fortune. For it was what we all know today as Bird's Custard.

Alfred Bird's love and concern for his wife was to make his name a household word.

THE FRIENDSHIP BOOK

Sunday—September 21.

THEREFORE thou shalt keep the commandments of the Lord thy God, to walk in his ways, and to fear him.

Monday—September 22.

I OFTEN scribble down sayings or thoughts that come my way. Let me share some of these with you.

When success turns your head, you could be looking at failure.

If you can't find a sunny side to your life, polish up the dark side.

Patience comes easiest to those who find something to do while they're waiting.

An optimist is a bridegroom who thinks he has no bad habits.

The grass may look greener next door, but it's just as hard to cut.

Everything is impossible to the person who doesn't try.

Tuesday—September 23.

SIX-YEAR-OLD Kenneth gave Granny a Bible for her birthday. He had chosen it himself, and he wanted to write a message inside the front cover. He knew that was the thing to do. His father had recently been given a book by a friend, and there on the fly-leaf he found what he was looking for.

Kenneth wasn't really sure what it meant, but he copied it very carefully into Granny's Bible, and showed it to nobody at all.

That was why, when Granny opened the Bible, she was surprised to read, " With the compliments and best wishes of the author."

THE FRIENDSHIP BOOK

Wednesday—September 24.

MRS SUSAN BERRIE helps her husband with his upholsterer's business.

Often, when chairs are being repaired, the odd coin will fall out on to the workfloor.

The Berries are not always sure which chairs they come out of, and at first they didn't know what to do with the coins. So they started a jar. Any money they found went into it. And when it was full they sent it to their favourite charity.

It's rather nice to think we may sometimes be contributing to a good cause without knowing anything about it!

Thursday—September 25.

HAVE you ever heard of a tuit—pronounced too-it?

I hadn't, until Mrs Anita Scott, of 64 Woodhall Place, Coatbridge, sent me one. She came across it in her church magazine. It offered one free to every reader—and a mighty fine thing these tuits seem to be. In fact, everyone with a problem should have one. The best, I'm told, are the round ones. They can help you in all sorts of ways, and are particularly useful for people who have been meaning to do something but haven't found the time.

You find it hard to believe? Well, that letter you meant to write, for example. They can help there. And with the plants that aren't in your garden yet. They'll speed the visit you've been meaning to make to an old friend. Even the word of praise you meant to give but somehow haven't mentioned. All these things, and many more, you can now accomplish quite easily.

If you don't believe me, try it for yourself. All you've got to do is get a round tuit!

HOME TOWN

*It's not the bricks and mortar
But the values handed down,
From age to age entrusted,
That create a living town.*

DAVID HOPE

THE FRIENDSHIP BOOK

Friday—September 26.

THE European Games held in Prague in 1978 gave television audiences the world over many nail-biting moments. But for those who witnessed it, one incident stands out in the memory. A young girl had just cleared the bar of the high jump and was leaping in the air with obvious jubilation when, after a pause, the bar behind her trembled and fell to the ground.

It meant the loss of a gold medal, and it was a moment of terrible disappointment for her, but instead of bursting into tears or showing annoyance she marched straight over to the girl who had won and warmly embraced her in congratulation.

She showed us that day what sportsmanship is all about.

Saturday—September 27.

SOMETIMES when I hear a person boasting I think of the composer, Haydn. At the age of 76, he attended a Gala performance of his oratorio " The Creation." At the end of one of the most rousing passages the audience broke into cheers and applause.

At first Haydn thought they were showing their appreciation of the music, but suddenly he realised they were applauding *him*. At once he rose to his feet and calmed them with his hand. " No — not from me, but from there, comes all," he said, pointing heavenwards.

Sunday—September 28.

I COMMAND thee this day to love the Lord thy God, to walk in his ways, and to keep his commandments.

THE FRIENDSHIP BOOK

Monday—September 29.

IT is said that Euclid, the famous Greek mathematician, once deeply offended his brother, who cried out in a rage, " Let me die, if I am not revenged on you one time or other !"

To which Euclid gently replied, " And let me die if I do not soften you by my kindnesses and make you love me as well as ever."

Tuesday—September 30.

COMING down the path one night I put my heel on an autumn leaf and nearly went my length on the ground.

So after tea I got out a rake and brush and set about doing some sweeping up. The Lady of the House came out, stood for a moment or two, picked up a leaf and started back in again.

When I asked what she was up to she told me she was looking for a richly-coloured leaf. " You can have a whole gardenful," I said with a sweep of my arm. " But why?"

" Well, Francis," she smiled, " if you must know, I'm going to press it in the hymn book at the Christmas carols."

I must have looked puzzled, for she went on, " Well, it's been a good summer, hasn't it? We've a lot to look back on and be grateful for. So I just thought—if I popped a leaf where we'll find it at Christmas, why, it will help tie up the year, so to speak."

I must say I smiled to myself, after she'd gone, but as I continued my sweeping in the gathering dusk I wondered if there isn't a parable in my lady and her autumn leaf.

Looking back *and* looking forward ! That surely is one of the secrets of a happy spirit.

OCTOBER

Wednesday—October 1.

ONCE again we have been singing that grand old harvest festival hymn by the 18th century German pastor Matthias Claudius, "We plough the fields and scatter the good seed on the land."

A grand hymn . . . But what nonsense it is! *We* don't plough the fields and scatter. Quite apart from the fact that few of us are farmers, just look at the average harvest festival display . . . food and fruits from all over the world. Just think how much we depend on harvests from other lands—India, Africa, Canada, the West Indies, the Middle East, and so on.

The harvest festival reminds us how dependent we are on each other and how we need to share out the fruits of the earth, making sure that no one goes hungry. As another well-loved harvest hymn reminds us, "All the world is God's own field."

Thursday—October 2.

WHEN the builders were at work on the first Eddystone Lighthouse in the summer of 1697, England was at war with France. A French privateer suddenly appeared, took the workers prisoner and sailed off with them to France.

The builders did not know what their fate might be, but, to their amazement, they were taken before King Louis XIV himself so that he could apologise to them. "I am at war with England," he said, "not with humanity." And he had them safely escorted back to the Eddystone Rocks so that they could complete their work on the much-needed lighthouse.

THE FRIENDSHIP BOOK

Friday—October 3.

A YOUNG teacher from the city had taken over a country school. In her first arithmetic lesson she decided to relate the sums to their own lives. She asked, " If there were five sheep in a field and two got through the fence, how many would be left?"

She was taken aback when one boy at once answered, " None, miss."

" Wrong," said the teacher. " Two from five leaves three."

" Oh, no, miss," the boy explained. " My dad's a shepherd. If two got through the fence the others would follow." Then with a seriousness beyond his years he went on, " Counting's one thing, miss, but I know about sheep."

Saturday—October 4.

HERE'S another selection from the ten-second sermons which sometimes come my way:

Your dreams may not come true—but neither may your nightmares.

A young man never realises that some day he'll know as little as his father.

If you want your friends to be perfect, you'll never have any.

An opportunist is someone who becomes successful doing today what *you* intended to do tomorrow.

If your work speaks for itself, don't interrupt.

Much of what we see depends on what we're looking for.

Sunday—October 5.

I WILL lift up mine eyes unto the hills, from whence cometh my help.

THE FRIENDSHIP BOOK

Monday—October 6.

EVERY year when autumn comes round I never fail to read that poem by John Keats—his famous " Ode to Autumn." How marvellously he expresses the delights of this " Season of mists and mellow fruitfulness."

Yet not everybody has an appreciation of poetry. I love the story of the rough sergeant-major who was announcing to his men on parade the subject of an education lecture. " It's a lecture on Keats," he barked out. " And you'd better all be present. I don't suppose any of you ignorant lot even knows what a keat looks like !"

Tuesday—October 7.

I'VE just been reading a light-hearted note from Mrs Grace Stirling, of 52 Durham Road, Kettering.

Like most of us, Grace has sometimes wondered what it feels like to be somebody outstanding. Perhaps to have a perfect voice, the ability to write a best-seller, to come up with something completely new or, if a woman, to be outstandingly beautiful.

Mrs Stirling tells me she thinks she knows that feeling.

How and where did she find it?

Well, she was simply tidying her wool bag with her two granddaughters. As the youngsters happily " helped," one whispered to the other. Her sister nodded. Then the two wee girls turned their faces up to Grace. They told her they were glad she was their granny because she was " the goodest granny in all the world."

Every granny will understand the warm glow that Grace felt at that moment. And why, though fame has passed her by, she knows its feeling.

THE FRIENDSHIP BOOK

Wednesday—October 8.

WORRIES always seem worse at night.
Lying awake in the dark, fancy takes over, the mind sees the worst. I'm thinking, as I write, of an elderly woman who lives alone in a large housing scheme. Old Mary has a lot on her mind. Many nights, to try to quell her anxiety, she gets up and makes herself a cup of tea. She finds it comforting to go through the routine of boiling the kettle and filling her cup. Her troubles seem less, somehow, and as she looks out of her kitchen window she sees other pinpoints of light in the silent, sleeping world and she feels comforted by them.

Perhaps a young mother is up feeding her baby, or someone is returning from the nightshift. Maybe someone else, worried like herself, is also up making tea. The lights are proof to her that the world goes on, another day will come and they will live through it together.

Sometimes, as Mary goes back to her bed, she leaves her light on, to shine for someone else, who may look out their window as she did, and draw from it a little hope and consolation.

Thursday—October 9.

WILLIAM PLANT WOODCOCK was a much-loved and highly-successful doctor in Holcombe, near Bury. The opening of the railway in those parts in 1846 was a great boon to him, enabling him to travel quickly into Bury and to Manchester. It was noticed that he always travelled third class—which one day prompted someone to ask him why, especially when his son John travelled *first* class.

After a moment's thought he replied, " Ah, well, you see, John has a rich father—I haven't !"

THE FRIENDSHIP BOOK

Friday—October 10.

A LITTLE boy had become an uncle at the age of four and was taken to see the new baby for the first time.

"What's she saying, Sandy?" asked his sister, as the infant made the usual gurgling noises.

Sandy glanced warily around the room, and then replied, "She's saying: 'Give Sandy an apple.'"

Saturday—October 11.

TOWARDS the end of the war the south coast of England was under fire from what we called "doodlebugs." When the flying-bomb's engine cut out you knew it would dive to earth in a few moments.

The W.V.S. had just started a makeshift meals-on-wheels service. A team were going round distributing sandwiches and cups of tea to old people. When the air raid siren went everybody made for the shelter. All except for one young girl, who protested that Miss Willison, a housebound old lady, always expected her before one o'clock.

Five minutes later there was that awful silence as the doodlebug fell—a direct hit on Miss Willison's house. When the bodies were taken from the rubble the young W.V.S. girl was laid on the grass. In her lifeless grasp was the handle of a broken cup —the cup she had been about to give Miss Willison when the bomb struck.

I find that symbolic of the service and sacrifice of the great W.V.S. team.

Sunday—October 12.

SEARCH me, O God, and know my heart: try me, and know my thoughts.

THE FRIENDSHIP BOOK

Monday—October 13.

AT the turn of this century two teenage brothers had just failed their exams. Needing money badly, they advertised for sale the books they had used for their studies. To their surprise, they received many replies. This gave them an idea. They combed second-hand bookshops for other copies of the books they'd offered, and thus they ended up with a modest but much-needed profit.

But they didn't stop there. They went on buying books and reselling, opened a shop and worked fifteen hours a day to make it a success. Soon William and Gilbert Foyle were running the largest book shop in London. Today, Foyle's Bookshop in Charing Cross Road is world famous. I never pass it without thinking of the two young men who turned failure into success.

Tuesday—October 14.

SOME foreign sailors were shipwrecked on a small island. They were treated with great kindness and hospitality, and in gratitude they taught the islanders a beautiful and intricate knitting pattern. The sailors were from the Spanish Armada, and the island was Fair Isle—the name the pattern bears to this day.

Another traveller who left his mark was Brendan, the Irish saint, who carried the message of Christianity to Scotland and Brittany. Besides spreading the Gospel, it is said that he also left behind this little prayer, " Oh, God, help me, for my boat is so small and Your sea is so great."

The Spanish sailors left a beautiful knitting pattern. Brendan left the word of God and a brief but telling prayer. What sort of mark will we leave to the world?

THE FRIENDSHIP BOOK

WEDNESDAY—OCTOBER 15.

I KNOW there's really nothing new to be said about autumn, but Violet Hall of Calne, Wiltshire, says it all in an attractive way in her *Song of Gold*:

The harvest fields, now painted gold
  With seas of ripened wheat,
Mark time with sigh of drifting leaves,
  That gather round my feet.

A blackbird pecks at russet fruit,
  Then from its throbbing throat,
There pours a liquid melody,
  With gold in every note.

September pipes a mellow tune,
  When summer, past recall,
Yields up her wealth on autumn's breath,
  A song of gold, for all.

THURSDAY—OCTOBER 16.

WHEN Sir Winston Churchill resigned the Premiership in 1955, one of his colleagues, R. A. B. Butler (now Lord Butler) sent him a letter of appreciation.

He thanked Sir Winston for having given him inspiration and the strength to face moments of crisis. He ended his letter with this quotation from St Augustine:

Let nothing disturb thee,
Let nothing affright thee,
All passeth away,
God alone will stay,
Patience obtaineth all things.

Mr Butler added, " This is what I, like St Augustine, have learned."

THE FRIENDSHIP BOOK

Friday—October 17.

IN the pulpit of All Hallows Church, the famous John Wesley once discovered that he had forgotten his sermon—he had left it at home. Nervous and upset, he left the pulpit and was going into the vestry when an elderly woman asked him what was wrong. When he told her, she exclaimed, " Is that all? Cannot you trust God for a sermon?"

John Wesley took her at her word, went back into the pulpit and preached with such power that he never afterwards took a written manuscript into any pulpit.

Saturday—October 18.

SOME years ago a man set out for a country walk and lost his way. On a lonely track he came upon a cottage and decided to ask for directions. With quiet courtesy an elderly woman invited him in for a cup of tea and a home-baked scone.

He was taken aback to see how simply she lived and how barely her room was furnished—just a table, two wooden chairs and an old iron bedstead in the corner.

" You seem so content, yet you have so little," he said. " Where is all your furniture?"

" Where is yours?" she said with a smile.

" Mine?" echoed the traveller in surprise. " Why should I have any here? I'm just passing through !"

The old woman smiled again. " So am I," she said quietly.

Sunday—October 19.

HE that hath two coats, let him impart to him that hath none; and he that hath meat, let him do likewise.

THE FRIENDSHIP BOOK

Monday—October 20.

I HAVE just been admiring, in the magnificent Norman abbey at Selby in Yorkshire, a beautiful stained glass window behind the high altar. It dates from the 14th century, and its beautiful colours are a truly marvellous sight.

But the window is a marvel in another sense. On the night of October 19, 1906, fire broke out in Selby Abbey, and soon the building was blazing from end to end. The great east window was saved from damage by a simple act of dedication. A team of firemen kept the glass cool by playing their hoses on it throughout the long night.

These men are not mentioned in the guide books, and I suppose nobody even remembers their names. Yet by simply doing their duty they preserved a priceless heritage for generations to come.

Tuesday—October 21.

NOWADAYS, people don't think twice about crossing the Atlantic at 700 m.p.h., but I remember hearing about the first non-stop trans-Atlantic crossing in June 1919. A Vickers-Vimy biplane, piloted by John Alcock, with Arthur Whitten Brown as his navigator, flew from Newfoundland to Ireland where weather conditions made them land.

Brown later wrote about their exploit in an article entitled, " Flying the Atlantic in Sixteen Hours." But what Brown did not reveal was that, at one point, he had climbed out on to the wing at a height of 11,000 feet in the middle of a storm to chip away the ice that was blocking essential tubes and freezing the instruments.

It was John Alcock who described that feat by his courageous and modest co-pilot.

FIRST THINGS FIRST

Even amidst the frost and snow,
The swans about their business go
Never beyond the present thinking,
Heedless of how the pond is shrinking.

*Now you and I—do we worry too much
About banks and bills and houses and such?
Happiest we when our needs are few
Like the ways of men when the world was new.*

DAVID HOPE

THE FRIENDSHIP BOOK

Wednesday—October 22.

MANY a wedding guest dwells for a moment on how the mother of the bride must be feeling.

But fathers, ahh . . . after a joke or two about being bankrupted by the festivities they take a bit of a back seat. Well, I had a letter from a father whose daughter was married recently. In it he captured what a lot of fathers feel.

"*It is my daughter's wedding day. I feel both glad and sad. My little girl is twenty now; how quick the years we've had. Her sunny smile and laughing eyes, how fast they banished care when I came home from work each night, and she was waiting there. She could twist me round her finger, and I didn't mind a bit—a willing prisoner of her charm, I'd go along with it. I have memories of holding her, just a few minutes old. A toddler with her teddy bear, how the scenes unfold—into pictures of her growing years, schoolgirl with hockey stick, then sitting up till all the hours when in the boy friends tripped.*

"*Today she can cry, my wife can cry with tears they needn't save. But I just smile and nod and wave, and in my heart my thoughts must hide—for whoever heard of crying from the father of the bride?*"

Thursday—October 23.

I LIKE a good argument, especially when I can discuss some worthwhile subject with someone who sincerely holds a different point of view. There are certain ideas, though, which can never really be defended by reason. We either accept them or we do not.

When I get on to such matters of faith I often think of some words written by Blaise Pascal, the great French Christian thinker : " The heart has its reasons, of which reason knows nothing at all."

THE FRIENDSHIP BOOK

Friday—October 24.

THE pupils at a Lancashire school were asked in the course of a written test: " Name the man or woman with whom you would most like to be stuck in a lift."

One smart miss wrote: " The lift man."

Saturday—October 25.

AS I stepped out the door this morning the cold wind made me shiver. It made me think about the paper boys and girls, milkmen and postmen—all out much earlier than I am, making the morning routine more pleasant for the rest of us.

Strangely, the first letter I opened was about someone who used to do just that, Syd Rook, who delivered the papers in the village of Great Orton, near Carlisle. It was a long round, for the houses and farms are scattered, but Syd was never without a smile as bright as the woolly hat he always wore.

No matter how pushed for time he was, Syd always had a minute for a cheery chat. Not only that, when the price of vegetables shot up a year or two ago Syd extended his vegetable garden. Hardly a morning passed without two or three old folk finding a grand turnip, a lovely cabbage or a beetroot that Syd had left on their step.

Syd has retired now. The village misses him and his morning sunshine. So theirs is a tribute I'm happy to pass on. But it's more than that. For Syd Rook, the paper man, shows what one pair of hands and a cheerful heart can accomplish . . .

Sunday—October 26.

DO good, O Lord, unto those that be good, and to them that are upright in their hearts.

THE FRIENDSHIP BOOK

Monday—October 27.

ONE of the many famous comedians to come from Liverpool is " Big-hearted " Arthur Askey. Once he was asked why the city of Liverpool had produced so many comedians. Instantly he replied, " Because you've got to be a comedian to live in Liverpool!"

Of course, it was a joke—but with a grain of truth behind it. A sense of humour helps us to put up with all sorts of things that otherwise would get us down. In Liverpool they've learned better than most how to laugh at their troubles. It's a lot better than crying over them!

Tuesday—October 28.

*IT wasn't much that I had done,
  But Tom said, " That was grand."
We'd had a chat, and when I left
I gripped him by the hand.
A small thing, really, I had done
But when you're ill and old
A friendly call from one who cares
Is worth far more than gold.*

Wednesday—October 29.

ANYONE who's ever been in a hospital will appreciate this little story.

Two little boys in a children's ward were discussing their hospital experiences.

" Are you medical or surgical?" one asked.

" I don't know what you mean," said the other.

The first boy, who had been a patient in the ward for some time, looked scornfully at the newcomer.

" Were you ill when you came," he explained, " or did they make you ill once you got here?"

THE FRIENDSHIP BOOK

Thursday—October 30.

THIS is the parable of the gossip and the goose feathers.

It comes to me from Mrs J. Scott, who lives in San Francisco, that mighty American city which takes its name from Francis of Assisi.

It seems a woman once went to Francis and told him she had been spreading nasty gossip about neighbours. Now her conscience was bothering her. How far could such gossip go, she wondered, and was there any way she could undo its harm?

Francis thought for a moment, then told the woman to go home and pluck a goose. He instructed her to go round the village and lay a feather at the door of each neighbour about whom she had passed on a wounding story. Finally, he said, go back to where you began and start to pick up all the feathers.

The woman set off, but by the time she returned to the first door, the wind had scattered the feathers beyond recall, all over the village . . .

Friday—October 31.

HERE'S a story to end the month with a smile. It's about a thrifty Aberdonian, newly arrived in London and waiting for a bus.

When the bus drew up at the stop he asked the conductor, " What's the fare from here to Trafalgar Square?"

" 12p," said the conductor. So the Aberdonian stepped back and ran on to the next stop.

" How much from here?" he asked. " Still 12p," replied the conductor.

The Aberdonian legged it to the next stop.

" How much now?" he asked breathlessly.

" 15p," replied the conductor with a smile. " You're running the wrong way."

NOVEMBER

Saturday—November 1.

WHEN I get home late the Lady of the House always has a cup of tea waiting for me. The other night, she had a story for me, too. She had been reading how the first cup of tea was made.

In China nearly 5000 years ago, water was not safe unless it was boiled. Since boiled water is not the sort of thing you'd drink by choice, someone tried adding the dried, chopped leaf of the tea plant, simply to make it taste better!

Since then, of course, tea has become part of our way of life. It is drunk when friends get together, when life becomes a little too much to cope with, when problems beset us, when bad news reaches us.

We make new friends over a cup of tea, and keep old ones with its help. Where would we be without it?

Sunday—November 2.

I WAS glad when they said unto me, Let us go into the house of the Lord.

Monday—November 3.

YOUNG Kenneth was very keen to have a baby brother or sister. He kept asking his mother why they couldn't get one. After all, his pal's mother got one. His mum explained that they couldn't afford one at present, but perhaps later . . .

One day Kenneth came home from school in great excitement.

"Come on, Mum," he cried. "There's a notice outside the church hall—'All Welcome—Children half-price.'!"

THE FRIENDSHIP BOOK

Tuesday—November 4.

MOST people know that the moving words of "Abide With Me" were written in the face of serious illness by Henry Francis Lyte, vicar of the Devonshire village of Lower Brixham. Less well known is the fact that the tune to which we always sing the hymn "Eventide" was also written during a time of great sorrow. The composer was Dr W. H. Monk, editor of the first music edition of *Ancient and Modern*.

Dr Monk and his wife had just lost their little daughter, only three years old. Mrs Monk later described how the grieving parents gained comfort each day by watching "the glories of the setting sun." One evening, she tells us, her husband was inspired to write some music. "As the last golden ray faded he took up some paper and pencilled that tune which has gone all over the world."

When both words and music were written as a triumph over suffering, no wonder that this hymn has given strength to millions.

Wednesday—November 5.

I'VE just been to a bonfire party. What a tremendous blaze we had! All those branches and old planks and bits of rubbish roaring away like an inferno. Yet it was all started by the tiny flame from a single match.

The remarkable way in which fire spreads was noted by St James in his epistle. "Behold how great a matter a little fire kindleth!" Do you remember what he used this to illustrate? It was the harm which can be done by a single wagging tongue, setting off the spreading fire of gossip . . . How we need to watch what we say—and guard our tongues, just as we guard a fire!

THE FRIENDSHIP BOOK

Thursday—November 6.

ON Remembrance Day a poppy wreath is placed on the war memorial that stands on the little hillock in the centre of Newtonmore, Inverness-shire.

But this story is about a wreath that once lay there, and the little girl who stole a poppy from it. She was only four, and while her parents were looking in the window of a nearby shop, she and her big sister climbed the steps to the war memorial. There they found the wreath, faded, but still garlanded with poppies, and before her elder sister could stop her, the child had reached out a hand and taken a flower.

Of course, she didn't know any better. But when she brought it proudly to her parents, her father was not pleased, and told her firmly she should not have touched the wreath. That's when a small, grey-haired woman spoke. She had been standing nearby, and had overheard everything.

"Don't scold her," she said in a soft, Highland voice. "She wasn't to know." She paused, and went on, "My husband's name is on that stone. If he'd come back, we might have had a bairn just like yours." She smiled, and added, "Let her keep that poppy for him—he'd have liked to think his flower could make a little girl happy."

A stolen poppy, a widow's longing, a child's joy, and a soldier's death. Somewhere, in all of these, lies the true meaning of Remembrance Day.

Friday—November 7.

FRIENDSHIP, like a lovely jewel,
  Glows brightly through the years.
A handshake firm, a gentle smile,
  Can chase away all fears.

THE FRIENDSHIP BOOK

Saturday—November 8.

EVERY Boy Scout knows he has to "Be Prepared." Perhaps the man was a former Scout who erected this sign on a stall in a London street market:
"Sunshades For Sale—Guaranteed Waterproof!"

Sunday—November 9.

BE strong and of a good courage, fear not, nor be afraid . . . for the Lord thy God, he it is that doth go with thee.

Monday—November 10.

I BUMPED into a doctor friend the other day.
As we stood chatting at the edge of the pavement a youngster of eight came trotting up to him. With a smile the boy pulled a boiled sweet out of his pocket and offered it to him. "It's my last one, Doctor," he said nobly, "but you can have it."

Well, the fingers that held the sweet were decidedly grubby. The boiling itself was dusty and gritty, and looked as if it had been in the boy's pocket for some time. But my friend smiled gratefully to his young patient. "Thanks, Tommy," he said—and popped the sweet into his mouth, while Tommy went proudly on his way.

The doctor chuckled as he watched him go. Then he turned to me. I knew what we were both thinking. That sweet could not be very hygienic. But he laughed.

"There are times when it's really more blessed to receive than to give—indeed, now and again, receiving can be a bigger sacrifice than giving!"

And, with a wink, off he strode, sucking young Tommy's sweet as he went!

THE FRIENDSHIP BOOK

Tuesday—November 11.

THE Lady of the House and I were at a wedding.
We've known Lorraine's family for many years. Of course, all eyes were on her as she came down the aisle, a perfect picture. More so, I think, because she was on the arm of her brother. Her father, a man dearly loved by all his family, had died not long before after a long and painful illness.

Manfully, Lorraine's brother fulfilled his duty of giving his sister away, then slipped into the pew beside his mother. I am sure everyone in the church felt a hint of sadness at that moment. I confess that as we rose to sing the bridal hymn " O Perfect Love . . . the love which knows no ending," my eyes strayed to the pew where mother and son stood alone—mother thinking of the days that had been for her and her husband, and would be no more, and, as every mother must, thinking, too, of the years ahead for her daughter.

As we sang, I saw the young man quietly enfold his mother's hand in his, quite firmly, and press it. If ever one picture was worth a thousand words, that gentle handclasp was for me.

I know every woman will understand the significance of this story, and I cannot but believe we all gain something from sharing its silent message.

Wednesday—November 12.

WAIT before you worry,
Wait before you frown,
Don't let any problems of
The future get you down;
Wait before you give up hope
Because a plan went wrong,
Wait, for something better
Will be sure to come along.

THE FRIENDSHIP BOOK

Thursday—November 13.

BEN DRANSFIELD is the headmaster of a little school in the peaceful English countryside, but he often looks back to the time when he led a busy and sometimes adventurous life as an education officer in remote parts of Uganda. He recently recalled an instance of the remarkable friendship shown to him by African colleagues.

One day he was on safari when he received a warning that there was a vicious hyena in the district, and he was advised to take extra precautions. That night he went to sleep in a small hut with no door. When he woke in the morning he was moved to see his African colleague lying asleep—across the open doorway so that he might protect him from possible danger.

There can be no greater friendship than that of a man who is prepared to lay down his life for his friend.

Friday—November 14.

A FRIEND who has been travelling in the Far East tells me that when he arrived at Hong Kong he was handed a book of " cheques " issued by the Hong Kong " Bank of Courtesy."

If he went into a shop and received exceptionally good service he wrote the details on one of the " cheques." The shopkeeper sent the " cheque " to the island's Tourist Association. Each month shopkeepers receive rewards according to the number of cheques they return.

I don't suppose even the prospect of rewards will ever turn an unhelpful shopkeeper into a helpful one. But what a good idea to give a bit of recognition to those who are taking trouble to please their customers !

THE FRIENDSHIP BOOK

Saturday—November 15.

DAVID WILSON is only 38, yet he is so badly crippled by arthritis that he is unable to work. But he can still manage to swim, and so one day recently he decided he would raise some money —not for victims of arthritis but for the special baby care unit of his local hospital.

You see, a few years ago this unit saved the life of David's new-born baby. So, after a send-off kiss from his son Matthew—now a healthy four-year-old—David Wilson went into the water to swim 50 lengths for which his sponsors paid a total of £75. How easily he could have sat back and let others raise the money . . . But it was something he had to do, a debt of gratitude he had to repay.

Sunday—November 16.

THY word is a lamp unto my feet, and a light unto my path.

Monday—November 17.

A MINISTER was invited by his neighbour, a priest, to pay him a visit. As the priest showed him round his large, well-furnished room the minister could not help thinking of his own rather shabby vicarage and how his wife struggled to keep looking reasonably respectable.

As the priest showed him out at the end of the visit he asked the minister, " Well, what do you think of it?"

The minister thought for a moment. " It's very nice," he said. And then he smiled. " Perhaps you priests have better quarters than we do—but we ministers do have better halves !"

THE FRIENDSHIP BOOK

Tuesday—November 18.

THERE are so many ways of saving advertised today that some of us probably forget that not so long ago many people did not trust banks but found some hiding place for what they could save.

A reader tells me that her Scots granny hid her money in an old purse in one of her stockings, and whenever a bill had to be paid she would disappear into her bedroom and reappear with the cash. Sometimes the purse would work itself down and appear as a lump in her stocking.

It became known as " granny's sair (sore) leg,"— a well-loved joke in the family. " How's your sair leg today?" would arouse concern and sympathy in a visitor or stranger, while the family would wink and smile. Granny took it all in good part, and by means of her "sore leg" sent one son to university and set up another in business.

Wednesday—November 19.

MOST people know the famous painting of Christ knocking on the door of a house and saying, " Behold I stand at the door and knock." We are told on good authority that when the artist had completed this painting he brought his young son into the studio to view it.

The lad gazed intently for a while at the new picture and then shook his head. " It's great—but there's one mistake. You've forgotten something."

His father frowned. " What have I forgotten?"

" You've forgotten to put a latch on the door! Nobody could get in!" exclaimed the lad.

" Oh, no," replied his father, quietly. " There *is a latch on the door—but it's on the inside!*"

It was the artist's way of showing that only you and I can open the door to Him.

LONG AGO

How did they live, what did they think,
Those old lost peoples long gone under?
We can but guess, though what they left
Can fill us still with awe and wonder.

DAVID HOPE

THE FRIENDSHIP BOOK

Thursday—November 20.

Today I had a mixed bag of post. First there were one or two nice letters from friends, one containing some very good news. Then there was a circular, an Income Tax form, and a couple of bills —one of them a real shock! Finally, there was a letter bringing rather sad news.

When I had finished reading my mail I decided that here was a parable of life. Each day brings us a mixed bag of experiences, some good, some not so good, and some really unpleasant. And we simply have to learn to take the rough with the smooth. It's no use my asking the GPO only to deliver the good news. If the letters are addressed to me I have to accept them!

Friday—November 21.

Silver-haired Janet, a retired schoolmistress, loved social functions. Despite her age she rarely turned down an invitation to attend such gatherings where she was always made most welcome because her sense of humour delighted everybody.

On one occasion Janet announced that she was planning to give a party to mark her coming eightieth birthday and that she would invite scores of guests.

A friend asked teasingly, " Will you have a birthday cake, Janet?"

" Of course."

" And candles?"

" My dear," replied Janet, " it's a birthday party, not a torchlight procession!"

A frivolous remark? Yes. But it indicates a zest for living, a refusal to accept old age as an empty, dreary kind of existence. People like Janet do us all a power of good.

THE FRIENDSHIP BOOK

Saturday—November 22.

ELIZABETH TWISTINGTON-HIGGINS has been paralysed from the neck down for 26 years, but her story is one of bravery and determination. She has painstakingly learned how to paint, holding the brush between her teeth, and she now designs her own Christmas cards for the Mouth and Foot Painting Artists' Association. Before she was ill, Elizabeth trained at Sadler's Wells as a ballet dancer, and now she trains girls herself and has her own ballet dance group.

Elizabeth paints with her mouth and a prayerful heart, while others use praying hands to help and support her.

Sunday—November 23.

BLESSED be he that cometh in the name of the Lord.

Monday—November 24.

MIRIAM EKER, of Longsight, Manchester, sent me these lines :
*There's joy in going an errand,
In walking along the street,
In having a word of greeting
For the people that I meet.
There's joy in using a duster,
In keeping the doorstep clean,
In fixing on my windows
Bright curtains to be seen.
There's joy in doing the washing,
In cooking, and sweeping the floor
And I thank, thee, Lord, for
  the blessing
Of health to do each chore.*

THE FRIENDSHIP BOOK

Tuesday—November 25.

ON November 25 we celebrate St Catharine's Day.

Catharine was a king's daughter, a Christian girl who dared to denounce the Roman Emperor Maximinus to his face. For this " crime " she was scourged and thrown into prison. Whilst in prison she converted the Empress who had come to reason with her. The Emperor then commanded that Catharine be broken on a toothed wheel.

It is said that as soon as the wheel touched her it shattered into pieces. The brave girl met her death by the executioner's axe instead. Every Guy Fawkes' Day numerous catherine wheels are lighted in fireworks displays—a strange way of remembering her Christian witness and death.

Wednesday—November 26.

SUSAN, who has a young family, was weighed down with a bulging shopping bag when I met her homeward bound the other day. But she was smiling as if she hadn't a care in the world.

" Oh, yes, it's heavy," she said when I remarked on it. " But I'm glad of it ! "

She told me that one morning she had struggled on to a bus with a load of shopping and started to grumble about it to the elderly woman in the next seat. " She listened to me in silence and then, quietly, she said, ' I used to shop for my family, too. Now I'm on my own. This is all I need.'

" I looked at her thin little bag with its few items," said Susan, " and suddenly I realised how lucky I am. Perhaps some day I'll be shopping only for myself. Meantime I thank God I have a family to care for."

And off she went with a bright " Cheerio ! "

THE FRIENDSHIP BOOK

Thursday—November 27.

SPONSORED walks are very much in fashion these days. I think the most impressive one I have ever come across is Eddie Fischer's " Walk for Water," during which he tramped a total of 4100 miles.

In 1976 Eddie was doing relief work amongst the earthquake victims of the Rabinal Valley in Guatemala. He was so struck by the desperate need for a proper water supply and a system of irrigation that he decided to raise the necessary 300,000 dollars by walking all the way to his home in Newtown Square, Pennsylvania. He was met by his brother on the Texas border, and eventually they completed the journey and raised enough money for Eddie to return to Gautemala to install the system in March 1978.

Eddie Fischer has explained his achievement by saying that he was sustained throughout his gruelling journey by his religious beliefs. Those who think that faith is something vague and airy-fairy might do well to ponder on the fact that it helped Eddie to wear out twelve pairs of shoes doing what he knew to be right.

Friday—November 28.

IT was a foggy night and little Lisa knew her father would be late driving home.

At bed-time, when Lisa was kneeling at her bed saying her prayers, she asked, " And, God, please bring Daddy safely home through the fog." Just then the front door opened and her daddy called up the stairs, " Hullo, everyone, it's me."

Lisa opened her eyes for a moment, then closed them again. " Thank you, God," she said. " That was really quick !"

THE FRIENDSHIP BOOK

SATURDAY—NOVEMBER 29.

ON a bleak, dark night in 1943 a young German prisoner of war wandered through the streets of Catrine in Ayrshire. He was on special release to a local farm. In the distance he could hear the rumbling of Flying Fortresses, and Anton Shulte's heart ached as he thought of his family and friends back home and how futile the war was. Then the noise of the planes was drowned out . . . by the sound of hymn-singing from the Gospel Hall.

Anton nervously opened the door and slipped inside. He was given a warm welcome, and though he didn't know the words of the hymn, he found himself humming the tune.

Somehow he felt happy and secure for the first time in years, and there and then he vowed that once the war was over he would return to Germany and become an evangelist. After the service he was invited to the home of William McPhee in Mauchline Road. Every Saturday and Sunday night from then on, Anton went to the gospel meeting, and then home with William for supper.

After the war, true to his word, he became an evangelist whose reputation spread all over Germany. Thousands of people flocked to his meetings, and he founded the first radio mission in Germany. His broadcasts go out over Germany, Spain, Portugal and Iron Curtain countries, too.

Anton has been called the Billy Graham of Germany. His name is a household word throughout Europe—and all because he heard the sound of happy voices one night in the Gospel Hall in Catrine.

SUNDAY—NOVEMBER 30.

BE still, and know that I am God.

DECEMBER

Monday—December 1.

WE cannot remind ourselves too often of this old Chinese proverb:

"*If there be righteousness in the heart, there will be beauty in the character;*

If there is beauty in the character there will be harmony in the home;

If there is harmony in the home there will be order in the nation;

When there is order in each nation there will be peace in the world."

Tuesday—December 2.

THE Swedish racing-car driver, Gunnar Nilsson, had a most promising future. Having won the Grand Prix in Belgium at the age of 28, it looked as though he was certain to be a world champion.

Then he developed cancer, and within a year he was dead. But during that year he raised money to provide the latest cancer-fighting equipment, especially for the new Charing Cross Hospital. Even during the last week of his life he made scores of telephone calls and held bed-side meetings with those who were helping him towards his target of £350,000. In order to keep his mind alert he refused all pain-killing drugs. As one of his doctors said, "The totally unselfish expenditure of his remaining energies has commanded the respect of everyone in the hospital and all who knew him."

Great courage is needed to drive a racing car. Even greater courage to fight on in the face of illness and pain. As one newspaper headline put it, "Cancer Driver Dies—But He Wins His Last Race."

THE FRIENDSHIP BOOK

WEDNESDAY—DECEMBER 3.

MRS C. FRANCES ALEXANDER, who died in 1895, was one of the leading hymn-writers of her day. She wrote over 200 hymns, and many of these are still sung throughout the English-speaking world. Her famous *Once In Royal David's City* is immensely popular, especially at Christmas time.

But this gifted writer also had other interests. As the wife of a busy clergyman she frequently met all kinds of people, and it was the welfare of women, particularly of the working class, that always claimed her immediate attention. Not that she put on the Lady Bountiful act. Humbly she considered herself to be the friend and counsellor of any woman in need and distress. And in her quiet, gentle way she did wonderful work with lasting results.

Mrs Alexander had her critics, mainly among certain autocratic ladies who couldn't understand how she managed to deal so successfully with even the most difficult and tiresome cases. One day these ladies tackled her on the subject.

Mrs Alexander bowed graciously and quoted the words of the 17th century French mystic, Francis of Sales : " You will win more people by offering them a spoonful of honey than a jar of vinegar."

THURSDAY—DECEMBER 4.

ONE day Lord Kelvin, the famous scientist, was busy making a machine for taking soundings in the ocean. A friend noticed that he had a coil of piano wire, and asked him what it was for.

" For sounding," replied the scientist.

" What note?" asked his friend, with a twinkle in his eye.

Lord Kelvin, who had a great interest in music, answered, " Deep C !"

THE FRIENDSHIP BOOK

Friday—December 5.

HAVE you ever heard of the Brown Baggers? I hadn't until I came across an account of a small group of retired people in Salinar, California. This is a rich agricultural district, but there are many needy families, so the Brown Baggers decided to see what they could glean from the harvest fields. Armed with cheap brown bags—hence the name—they combed the fields and vineyards to see what had been left behind of no commercial value. Working in twos and threes, they eventually accumulated vast quantities of small but good quality grapes, potatoes, turnips, cabbages and vegetables of all kinds. The first load amounted to seven tons—enough to feed a hundred hungry people.

Inspired by the Old Testament story of Ruth gleaning in the fields of the Holy Land, the Brown Baggers have set a fine example of how to combine " waste not, want not " with valuable service to the community.

Saturday—December 6.

A LONG time ago two artists, Franz and Albrecht, lived together. Franz went out to do manual work while Albrecht worked at home and sold his paintings. One day Franz came home from work and described something to Albrecht with his work-worn hands. " Hold your hands there," said Albrecht, " I am going to paint them."

Poor Franz wondered why his friend should want to paint his rough old hands, but instead of hiding them he put them together as Albrecht wished, and so it was that Albrecht Durer gave to the world Franz's work-worn hands. The now famous painting, " The Praying Hands," has inspired Christians through the ages.

THE FRIENDSHIP BOOK

Sunday—December 7.

THE Lord shall preserve thy going out and thy coming in from this time forth, and even for evermore.

Monday—December 8.

DEAN HOLE once told a story of a young curate who was preaching in a strange church from which the rector was away. He preached a very short sermon, and in the vestry afterwards the church warden remarked upon its brevity.

The curate told him he had not intended it to be so short; a puppy at his lodgings had got into his room and eaten half the sermon he had prepared. The church warden was silent for a moment, and then he said, " I should be much obliged if you could get our rector one of the same breed."

Tuesday—December 9.

EDWARD, aged 19 and a keen motorist, had been giving his mother her first driving lesson. She proved to be a nervous, uncertain learner, and it was clear that it would take some time before she grasped even the most elementary rules.

Edward was annoyed. He thought that the previous half-hour had been a sheer waste of time. His mother would never make a good driver. Later that day at tea-time he remarked that as the first lesson had gone so badly he would prefer not to continue with the arrangement. His father looked at him across the table and then said quietly, " Think of the wonderful patience your mother had when she was teaching *you* to walk."

Edward saw the point. Today his mother is an excellent driver, much praised for her skill.

JUST LOOK!

Is there a greater wonder
Than a tree on Christmas Night,
By eager hands transformed
Into shimmering delight?

DAVID HOPE

THE FRIENDSHIP BOOK

Wednesday—December 10.

My friend Jack had an addition to his family, a little sister for six-year-old Susan. When he told Susan the news she was thrilled. " Oh, Daddy," she said, " does Mummy know? Let's go and tell her !"

Thursday—December 11.

SERAPHIM FORTES is still remembered with affection in Vancouver, though it's well over 50 years since he died. He was a coloured man from Barbados, who worked as a hotel porter. Seraphim was too much of a mouthful, so everybody just called him Joe.

He loved children, and he loved swimming, and all his spare time was spent down on the beach where the children used to swim and play. Many's the boy and girl who learned to swim with Joe's ham-like fist gripping the back of a cotton bathing suit, and his deep, mellow voice ordering, " Kick yo' feet, chile, kick yo' feet !"

When children got into difficulties in the water it was Joe who fished them out, and he was credited with more than a hundred such rescues. Parents would send their offspring to the beach for the day with the command, " Now don't go away from where Joe is."

When the old negro died, the cathedral was packed for the memorial service. In a moment of inspiration the organist substituted for the funeral march a melody that appeared more fitting, and the old man's body was carried to his burial to the strains of " Poor Old Joe."

Over his grave stands a stone bearing the simple words, " Little children loved him." It's the epitaph Seraphim Fortes would have wished.

THE FRIENDSHIP BOOK

Friday—December 12.

CAN you imagine Christmas without Christmas trees? In Uganda there are no spruce trees, so banana trees are used to decorate the roads. The day before Christmas the trees are cut and replanted at the roadsides. Each person plants trees from his home to the next, and then everyone combines to plant trees to the main road and then to the church. The trees are then garlanded with wild flowers, the roads swept, the grass verges cut.

The village drums, which have been silent all year, are put in the sun to dry. This has the effect of tuning them in readiness for Christmas night.

These customs occurred in the past when a king was expected in a village or town, and now at Christmas they welcome the King of Kings.

Everyone looks forward to Christmas Day. In the local language the day is called Sebukulo, which means " The Greatest Day of All."

Saturday—December 13.

VOLTAIRE, the famous 18th century French writer, philosopher and wit, is generally thought of as a bitter cynic, who spent much of his time and energy attacking the French Government and the Roman Catholic Church. Yet Voltaire did some positive things. In particular, he was a champion of tolerance, with an outlook he summed up in words we might well put into practice today : " I disagree with what you say—but I'll defend to the death your right to say it."

Sunday—December 14.

THE stone which the builders refused is become the head of the corner.

THE FRIENDSHIP BOOK

Monday—December 15.

ECOLOGISTS tell us that not a leaf falls to the forest floor or a raindrop to the sea but it will affect the universe and space throughout all time.

What are you and I going to do today? In the sight of God every one of us is important, much more so than a leaf or raindrop. What we do today really does matter.

Tuesday—December 16.

A BEAUTIFUL story is told of how Beethoven composed his famous "Moonlight Sonata." One evening he was walking home through the streets of Bonn. As he passed a house he heard one of his own compositions being played. He went through the garden up to the casement windows and looked in. A girl was sitting at the piano playing, and as he watched, Beethoven realised that she was blind. He stepped in through the window.

"Let me play that for you," he said. Despite her surprise, the girl allowed him to play, and so perfect was his touch that she exclaimed, "I can only think that you must be Beethoven himself!"

"I am," he said.

For a long time he played to her. It grew dark, but to the blind girl the darkness made no difference. At last Beethoven rose to go. "Play me just one more piece," the girl pleaded. By this time it was dark with a full moon. Beethoven sat down at the piano which was so near the broad windows that the moonlight came slanting across the keys. "Listen," said Beethoven, "and I will play for you the moonlight."

And there and then, it is said, he composed and played the first rippling movement of what is perhaps the most famous sonata in the world.

THE FRIENDSHIP BOOK

Wednesday—December 17.

I CAME across this verse by R. L. Hendrick in an old almanac. It was for the year 1895, but I don't think it is in the least out of date:

I can't tell why we quarrel
With such facility,
Although no doubt,
If figured out,
This would the reason be:
Sweets without acids make
A tasteless cup.
And thus I know
We quarrel so
Just for making up!

Thursday—December 18.

THIS morning I met Betty on her way to the post. She was walking a little more stiffly than usual, I thought. But that's not surprising when you are in your eighties.

" I mustn't miss the post," she said, " or Elsie will wonder what has happened to the money. It's not much, of course, but I know it means a lot to her."

Then she explained that she was in the habit of sending Elsie an occasional postal order—but not out of charity.

" You see, many years ago we were students together. I had a very small grant and nothing to spare, whereas Elsie was quite well off in those days. And she helped me out, treated me to meals and little luxuries . . . So now that she is not so well off in her turn, I help her out when I can."

She caught the post all right, and then hobbled off home, happy to have paid off another instalment of her debt of gratitude.

GLORY

Autumn is the best of seasons,
* Rich in colours full of cheer:*
Bright with gold and bronze and copper—
* Crowning glory of the year.*

                    DAVID HOPE

THE FRIENDSHIP BOOK

Friday—December 19.

SIR FRANCIS DRAKE, of Armada fame, believed that there was no point in doing a job unless he was to put his heart and soul into it. Many of us tend to start with a certain amount of enthusiasm, but then our interest wanes, our determination falters, and somehow the job never gets finished. It is well to remember the words of Drake, as they first appeared in the quaint spelling of 400 years ago:

"There must be a begynning of any great matter, but the continewing unto the end, untyll it be thoroughly finished, yeldes the true glory."

Saturday—December 20.

I HAVE spoken with many people who have been suffering from disabilities of one kind or another and they all say one thing—whatever we are suffering from gets worse when we are unhappy, lonely or bored. It gets better when we expect a visit from a friend, are immersed in a job or look forward to some little treat.

I am not preaching a sermon about this. I only suggest that we help ourselves physically by trying to look on the bright side. Those of us who are lucky enough to be fit and well have it in our power to help those in pain and discomfort by doing the small things that mean so much—a visit, a telephone call, sending a bunch of flowers—anything that helps to raise the spirits when these are at a low ebb.

Sunday—December 21.

IT is better to trust in the Lord than to put confidence in man.

THE FRIENDSHIP BOOK

Monday—December 22.

Two men look out through the same bars:
One sees the mud, and one the stars.

THOSE lines came to mind when I heard the remarkable story of Richard Prasher. For 40 years Richard worked as a railway ganger. But while his workmates were taking a well-earned rest, Richard spent his breaks on the railway embankment searching for specimens of wild flowers.

Because of his knowledge of the embankment flowers, Richard, now over 80, is in great demand with schools, woman's guilds and wildlife societies as a lecturer.

Since his retirement several years ago he has spent every Thursday, rain or shine, gathering flowers from the embankment, pit bings and rubbish dumps within reach of his home at Dalry. He takes them to Kelvingrove Art Gallery and Museum in Glasgow, to fill vases for the ground-floor display. Experts reckon Richard's vases are the finest of their kind in any museum.

The man who can see beauty where few would dream of looking—yes, there's an inspiration!

Tuesday—December 23.

AMONGST the ancient laws of Wales is the recommendation: " Every habitation should have two good paths, one to its church, the other to its watering place." A simple rule for simple times.

Nowadays water is piped and many roads lead to many places, but our needs are sophisticated and not easily satisfied.

In olden times life was frugal, but the path which brought spiritual comfort and hope was kept clear. Would it were still so.

THE FRIENDSHIP BOOK

WEDNESDAY—DECEMBER 24.

PHILIP and Robbie were being put to bed by Grandma, who had come to stay for Christmas. They had had their baths and were busy saying their prayers while Grandma tidied up the bathroom.

Robbie, the younger, concluded his prayer with a list of the presents he wanted for Christmas, recited at the top of his voice.

" Quiet !" Philip exclaimed. " God isn't deaf !"

" No," replied the other, " but Grandma is !"

THURSDAY—DECEMBER 25.

PART of the pleasure of Christmas lies in the wonderful opportunity it provides for us to show our affection for family and friends by making them gifts—gifts which are not necessarily expensive. An African boy once brought, as a Christmas present for his teacher, a most beautiful sea shell. When she asked him where he had got it he told her he had gone to a beach several miles away to find it. " You should not have gone all that way to get a gift for me," said the teacher. " Long walk part of gift," the boy said simply. He understood better than many of us today the true meaning of Christmas.

FRIDAY—DECEMBER 26.

WELL, Christmas comes but once a year
And now it's past again,
For some it brought gifts, laughter, fun,
For others, heartache, pain.
Yet if, within you, you can keep
The Christmas message true,
Then is there comfort, hope and joy
To last the whole year through.

REWARDED

> It's good to climb until you stand
> Where time can never go,
> High in a winter's wonderland
> Of sun and shining snow.

DAVID HOPE

THE FRIENDSHIP BOOK

Saturday—December 27.

YOUNG Stephen belonged to a poor family in London. His father had been unemployed for a considerable time, and his mother rarely enjoyed good health. In the circumstances, however, it was a reasonably happy household, even though the boy often experienced hunger and was always shabbily dressed.

One Christmas, along with the other children of the neighbourhood, Stephen arrived at the annual school party. Everybody had a wonderful time—excellent food, music, prizes, balloons, games. For these youngsters it was a kind of fairyland.

At the end of the party each child was given a large paper bag of cakes to take home. Stephen, clutching his treasured parcel, was hurrying down the street when he noticed a thin, tired-looking man leaning heavily on his walking-stick. Stephen stopped and asked him, " Would you like to have some of my cakes? They're absolutely marvellous, and you'll enjoy them."

" No, no, but thank you," replied the man as he moved away.

Stephen smiled gently. " Well, then, a happy Christmas!"

A few days later Stephen's mother received a brief letter containing £20. It ran :

Please accept the enclosed Christmas gift. You have a very wonderful son. The schoolmaster gave me your address. God bless you all."

The letter was signed by a distinguished physician.

Sunday—December 28.

GLORY to God in the highest, and on earth peace, good will toward men.

THE FRIENDSHIP BOOK

Monday—December 29.

THE manse or vicarage is usually a regular port of call for vagrants, and the minister—or his wife—have to cope with all kinds of requests. I like the story about the minister's wife who opened the door to a tramp, and, feeling she ought to encourage him to do something for himself, asked, " Have you ever been offered any work?"

" Only once, ma'am," replied the tramp cheerfully. " Apart from that I've been shown nothing but kindness."

Tuesday—December 30.

IN a primary school in North Wales the teacher had been explaining to her young pupils that God is omnipotent, all-powerful. " He can do everything. Nothing is impossible to God."

There was a long silence. Then eight-year-old Archie raised his hand : " Please, miss, I know something that God can't do."

" And what is that?" asked the teacher, brightly.

" He can't please everybody !"

Wednesday—December 31.

DIETRICH BONHOEFFER was imprisoned by the Nazis for his courageous witness as a Christian pastor, and in 1945 he was hanged by the Gestapo. From prison he had smuggled out various letters and writings which proclaimed his radiant faith, including a poem written at the beginning of the very year of his death. Here is the last verse :

While all the powers of Good aid and attend us,
Boldly we'll face the future, be what it may,
At even, and at morn, God will befriend us,
And, oh, most surely on each New Year's Day!

Where the Photographs were taken

QUIET HAVEN — *Polperro, Cornwall.*
REMEMBER — *Nr. Towyn, Merioneth.*
OLD TIME — *York Minster, York.*
THE LESSON — *Carregeennin Castle, nr. Llandilo, Carmarthenshire.*
THE WAY AHEAD — *Neidpath Woods, Peebles.*
COLOURS — *Ambleside, Cumbria.*
EXPLORERS — *Windsor, Berkshire.*
TRUE SKILL — *Benover, Kent.*
GREAT DAYS — *Ombersley, Worcestershire.*
WILD BEAUTY — *Naunton, Gloucestershire.*
PLEASURES — *Harnham Hill, Salisbury, Wiltshire.*
FREEDOM — *Runswick Bay, Yorkshire.*
RURAL RETREAT — *Chilham, Kent.*
AGE AND BEAUTY — *Urquhart Castle, Loch Ness, Inverness-shire.*
FRIENDS — *Boxmoor, Hertfordshire.*
LEARNING — *Whitby, Yorkshire.*
HOME TOWN — *Tewkesbury, Gloucestershire.*
FIRST THINGS FIRST — *Nr. Ludlow, Shropshire.*
LONG AGO — *Westbury Whitehorse, on Bratton Hill, Wiltshire.*
GLORY — *Glencoyne Woods, Ullswater, Cumbria.*
REWARDED — *Glenshee, Perthshire.*

Printed and Published by D. C. Thomson & Co., Ltd.,
185 Fleet Street, London EC4A 2HS.
© D. C. Thomson & Co., Ltd., 1979.